SINGULAR (female) VOICES

ANNA REYNOLDS

Anna Reynolds has had over fifteen plays produced in the UK and internationally, including *Precious* (West Yorkshire Playhouse), *Wild Things* (Salisbury Playhouse), *Deep Joy* (Mercury Colchester), *Red* (Traverse Edinburgh), *Ring Road Tales* (Palace Theatre, Watford) and *Blue Sky State* (Mercury Colchester).

Her writing for film includes *Paradise* (BBC2). Her writing for opera includes *Push* (London and Aldeburgh).

Anna runs the UK's premier writing website, www.writewords.org.uk.

MOIRA BUFFINI

Moira's plays include *Blavatsky's Tower* (London Fringe); *Gabriel* (Soho Theatre, LWT Plays On Stage Award and Meyer-Whitworth Award); *Silence* (commissioned by the National Theatre Studio, produced by Birmingham Rep and Plymouth Theatre Royal, winner of Susan Smith Blackburn Prize); *Loveplay* (RSC); *Dinner* (National Theatre Loft, Wyndhams Theatre, nominated for an Olivier Award for Best New Comedy); *The Teacher* (National Theatre's National Headlines series); *The Games Room* (Focus Group at Soho Theatre) and *Doomsday Girl* (RSC).

Her writing for film includes *Melissa Malone* (BBC); *Presence* (Prospect/Film Four); the screenplay of *Gabriel* (Passion Pictures) and *Dybbuk Box* (Mandate Pictures).

Catherine Johnson was born in Suffolk and raised in the West Country. She left school at sixteen and worked in Debenhams, a fancy-dress shop, an office, a pub and a record shop. She wrote her first play when she was thirty.

Catherine's plays include *Rag Doll*, *Renegades*, *Where's Willy* and *Too Much Too Young* (Bristol Old Vic); *Boys Mean Business*, *Dead Sheep*, *Shang-A-Lang* and *Little Baby Nothing* (Bush Theatre, London); *Through The Wire* (National Theatre/Shell Connections) and the musical *Mamma Mia!* currently playing worldwide.

For TV she has written episodes of *Casualty*, *Love Hurts*, *Byker Grove*, *Gold* and *Linda Green*. She has also written TV screenplays *Rag Doll*, *Where's Willy*, *Sin Bin* and created the C4 series *Love In The 21st Century*.

Her awards include the Bristol Old Vic/HTV Playwriting Award, Thames Television Writer-In-Residence Award and Thames Television Best Play Award. She was nominated for a Tony Award for *Mamma Mia!*

Catherine has two children and lives in Bristol. She wrote *The Lost Art Of Keeping A Secret* after being accosted at a party by the actress Lesley Nichol.

Stewart Permutt's writing includes *Exclusive Yarns* (co-written with Gary Lyons, Palace Theatre, Watford, Comedy Theatre London and Channel 4); *The Lime Green Bag*, (broadcast on Carlton); and *Singular Women* (Edinburgh Festival, national tour and broadcast on Radio 4).

Other radio credits include *My Heart Belongs to Manny* and *Comic's Interlude*.

Other theatre credits include *Singular People* (Edinburgh Festival, the New End Theatre and King's Head Theatre, London); *Charlie Lavender* (Southwark Playhouse) and *One Last Card Trick* (Palace Theatre, Watford).

SINGULAR
(female)
VOICES

JORDAN
Anna Reynolds with Moira Buffini

THE LOST ART OF
KEEPING A SECRET
Catherine Johnson

UNSUSPECTING SUSAN
Stewart Permutt

NICK HERN BOOKS
London
www.nickhernbooks.co.uk

A Nick Hern Book

Singular (female) Voices first published in Great Britain as a paperback original in 2006 by Nick Hern Books, 14 Larden Road, London W3 7ST

Jordan copyright © 2006 Anna Reynolds and Moira Buffini
The Lost Art of Keeping a Secret copyright © 2006 Catherine Johnson
Unsuspecting Susan copyright © 2006 Stewart Permutt

The authors of these plays have asserted their moral rights

Typeset by Country Setting, Kingsdown, Kent CT14 8ES
Printed in Great Britain by Biddles, King's Lynn

A CIP catalogue record for this book is available from the British Library

ISBN-13   978 1 85459 917 9
ISBN-10   1 85459 917 8

Publisher's Note

Two years ago we published a volume of short plays for
performance by one actor – *Singular (male) Voices*. It had
flown in the face of what I believed – and largely still believe –
about plays involving just one performer: namely, that they are
difficult to publish for a variety of reasons. But that volume
was well received – albeit by a select readership. So I was
beginning to toy with the idea of a companion volume of plays
for performance by a single *actress*, when I saw, in June 2005, a
staging of *Unsuspecting Susan* at the Actor's Centre in Covent
Garden, London, prior to a short run in New York at the admirable
Theater 59E59. I remembered seeing a much earlier version in
1998 when it was just one element in a play consisting of five
monologues by Stewart Permutt staged on the Edinburgh Festival
Fringe. (It was called *Singular People* – hah!) But Stewart had
substantially reworked the one about the middle-aged, middle-
class woman with the disturbed son, and it was now a substantial
piece running at over an hour. Moreover, it was providing a
superb vehicle for Celia Imrie, for whom the part might have
been written – as several critics remarked. I was lucky to catch
it – and her – as I had missed the premiere two years earlier at
Dan Crawford's King's Head Theatre in Islington.

So here, clearly, was a prime candidate for the new volume.
Now I had to find two more. I sent messages to all the play
agents in London asking for suitable scripts – and read a lot of
plays as a result. One stood out, *The Lost Art of Keeping a
Secret* by Catherine Johnson, whom I knew of as the author of
several plays at the tiny, 80-seat Bush Theatre, more or less
opposite our offices in Shepherd's Bush, West London, but also
as the – now extremely rich – author of the book of the ABBA
musical, *Mamma Mia!* Somehow suitably, *The Lost Art* has
two protagonists, both played by the same actress, who have
widely divergent lifestyles, but who both, like poor, unsuspecting
Susan, have terrible trouble with their offspring . . . A pattern
was beginning to emerge, but I was still lacking a third play.

One of the agents had mentioned a play that I knew had been first staged years and years ago – in fact in 1992 – and I wanted the volume to contain plays that were up-to-the-minute. So I confess that I approached *Jordan* in a slightly negative state of mind. It's all the more of a testament to the play, then, that I was overwhelmed by it: its power not at all diminished by the decade or more that had elapsed since it had first emerged, winning a Best Fringe Play award from the Writers' Guild. And of course *Jordan* too is about a distressed mother, though 'distress' is rather too tame a word for the situation Shirley finds herself in . . .

I hope you are as impressed by the plays as I was, and that if you are a performer or a director you will want to stage them. In fact, as I write this, Catherine Johnson's play has still not been performed: talented and versatile actresses, take note!

NICK HERN
April 2006

IN THE SAME SERIES:

SINGULAR (male) VOICES

MONGOOSE
Peter Harness

COLD COMFORT
Owen McCafferty

BRAZIL
Ronan O'Donnell

JORDAN

Anna Reynolds with Moira Buffini

Other sins only speak; murder shrieks out.
The element of water moistens the earth,
But blood flies upwards, and bedews the heavens.
Cover her face. Mine eyes dazzle: she died young.

John Webster, *The Duchess of Malfi*

Character

SHIRLEY

Jordan was first performed at the Lilian Baylis Theatre, London, in March 1992, with the following cast:

SHIRLEY   Moira Buffini

Director and Designer   Fiona Buffini
Stage Manager   Vera Peace

The play was subsequently revived at BAC and the Gate Theatre, London in 1994, where it was produced by Rupert Gavin and Dan Coleman, with the following cast:

SHIRLEY   Moira Buffini

Director and Designer   Fiona Buffini
Lighting Designer   John Linstrum
Stage Manager   Sonia Gannon

Jordan won the Writers' Guild Award for Best Fringe Play in 1992.

*A plain room containing nothing but an oversized chair. On the
floor is a bottle of water, a large pot of yoghurt and an
oversized woman's magazine.*

Lights up on SHIRLEY. *She is in her early twenties, fashionably
dressed in vibrant colours.*

SHIRLEY. Once upon a time, there was a miller and he had a
beautiful daughter with skin white as snow, lips red as blood
and long golden hair. The miller was a boastful man, and he
went to the king of all the land and told a tale of how his
beautiful daughter could spin straw into gold. The king did not
suffer fools lightly, so he said to the miller, 'Bring me your
daughter and she shall spin for me. If she can make gold out of
straw, she shall be my wife. But if she fails, she shall die.' At
this the miller wept, for he loved his only daughter more than
life itself. But the girl was brought to the palace and locked in
a chamber full of straw. In the corner was a spinning wheel.
Alone, she picked up a handful of straw. As she felt it
crackling through her fingers, she knew it would never be gold.
'Oh, what shall I do?' she cried. 'For tomorrow I shall surely
die!'

And then she heard a voice behind her. 'What is the matter,
pretty maid?' She turned around and there was the smallest,
strangest man she had ever seen. He was grinning widely and
he had a beard down to his waist. 'Why are you crying?' he
said. So she told him. 'I must spin all this straw into gold. If
I do it, I will be queen. But if I don't, the king will forfeit my
life!'

The little man grinned wider. 'I can do it for you,' he said. 'But
in return you must give me something precious.'

'I'll give you anything!' cried the miller's daughter. 'Anything
I own!'

'Well, promise me your son, if you become queen,' said the
strange little man. 'Give me your firstborn.'

'Who knows what may happen?' thought the miller's daughter, for she had no son and certainly would never be queen. She agreed at once. So the mannikin sat down at the spinning wheel and singing through the night, he spun all the straw into gold.

When the work was done, as it began to grow light, he went towards the window. 'Farewell,' he said, and he disappeared. The room was glowing with gold. When the king saw this, he was dazzled. He knelt down before the miller's beautiful daughter and they were betrothed.

Pause.

I've come from a big, red-brick building. Tall, thin windows made of thick plastic. Slits. Noise of girls laughing. Radios. A constant smell of dinner. Outside, I see Londoners passing by, squinting up. Back gardens. Washing lines, knickers hanging up to dry. The pub across the road. Sky. Signs of normal life.

They brought me here this morning in a van. A chauffeur-driven, door-to-door service from nick to court. I thought it would be posh, like *Rumpole of the Bailey*, but the floor was dirty and one of the walls had paint peeling off. When I went to the toilet, someone had written a joke about a pervert and a chicken on the back of the door. There was a screw standing outside and she said it was no laughing matter.

She thinks I'm mad. She knows I'm from *Fraggle Rock*, you see. That's what they call my wing back at the nick and you carry it round with you everywhere you go. The Muppet House; the Nut Wing. My home.

Only none of us say we're living there. Nobody intends to be staying for long. 'I'll be out on Monday,' they say. 'Up in court next week. Got my trial. Be a walk-out.' Like industrial action. Just passing through, see.

She takes a cigarette out of her bag.

I moved in one year ago today. So I'm celebrating this anniversary with a real cigarette.

Only, I haven't got a fuckin' light.

Big deal, that. In here you get used to roll-ups, scratching around for dog-ends, making your day good if you get enough of other people's leavings for a rollie of your own. We get given a light, every hour, on the hour, on our wing. No matches of our own. Too many people too fond of fire, see.

I was so afraid of fire with you.

One night I fell asleep with a cigarette in my hand, burnt a hole in the sofa. When I woke, I was shaking.

Dad always smoked. Used a cigarette filter, said it saved the nicotine from reaching his lungs. What did he die of? Lung cancer. I was there at the end. We all were. Two brothers, one sister, and me, the runt, the last born. None of us speaking to each other because we had nothing to say. Dad's teeth and hands yellow, stained with the blood of his killer. I turned away. What could I say? I need a fag.

Weighing it up, Jordan, I'd choose cancer over doing life, really. Both terminal illnesses, eating you away from the inside. I've seen women do their sentences, lifers, and go out, near to the end, on a home leave, eyes dead, future disappeared long since. No one left on the out for them. Past wiped away like grime off a window.

I said to one, I said, 'Where did you go? Didn't you find nothing?' 'Nothing was exactly what I found,' she said. 'My past upped and left while I was scrubbing the floor of my cell.'

Pause.

People feel sorry for you when they know you've seen a kiddie die young. They think of the nine months you carried him unborn, hugging yourself with the secret of it, getting rounder and fatter and more expectant. I carried the secret of you everywhere I went. I smiled strangely at people I didn't know, wanting to shout out at them: 'He's all mine!'

I longed and longed for you to arrive and I talked to you as I lay helpless at nights, pinned under the weight of my huge belly.

There's no need to talk to them, because I have you. You're still here, inside me, just like you were before you were born, silent, listening, breathing me in.

I dig and I dig and I rip my memory into shreds and then try to piece it all together like a torn photograph, hoping somehow you'll understand. I'll understand. So I'm not worried about talking to you. It may well be a sign of madness, as they say. Mad or bad. Padded cell or punishment cell and in between there lies the grey area, the space where you just exist. Where you wait.

You get up, you peer at pale grass through slits, littered with unwanted food, pigeon shit, Tampax. Strange sounds, if you listen very carefully, or you hear your own breathing, your mind ticking over furiously, searching, searching, always searching and you realise that mad is better by far, because it's a place where you don't have to search any longer.

Someone comes and does it for you.

And they go away with their raised eyebrows, closed notepads and they find you a label, the nearest one to your condition. They pin it on you because, like you got to have a number in here, you got to have an illness. It's a standard one, so you have to try and adapt to it in your own individual way. There are variations on being psychopathic, being depressive, and being neurotic: if you're depressive you cut yourself up, if you're psychopathic you cut someone else up, and if you're neurotic you worry about whether you should be cutting up anything at all.

I am searching. They search. It's different. See, I never understood. Never grasped things until they'd passed me by . . . All you can make sense of is the past. The present you just live.

Today.

Today, Jordan, I'm waiting. I'm waiting for a man in a wig to make a judgement about me; about us. A man with a wig white as snow and robes red as blood. This one has a kind face; a Santa Claus face. But he doesn't smile.

All I see in the courtroom is a blur of faces. The prosecution a sharp eagle, my barrister a soft red circle of worry and his skinny clerk, nervously picking at a pimple on his neck. My mother, sitting in the gallery, clutching her bag.

The jury . . . I count them over and over. There are twelve. A nice round number. When I glance up, I catch them trying to pretend they aren't looking at me. Ordinary faces, faces in a crowd. A blur.

The officer with me tells me when to stand and when to sit. Like church, only I'm not sure what religion. She's looking at me all the time, I can feel her eyes on the side on my face like heat but I don't look at her. When they lead me out, she puts her hand on my arm like I am blind.

When they come and get me it'll be for the last time. The waiting will be over. And then I'll know.

Pause.

When you're arrested, everything is bright. Bright, bright light; poking into your dark shadows. Hurts.

They sit you under a bulb while they take your photo. I smiled. Don't smile, they said crossly. It's not permitted.

She turns to the left.

This is my best profile.

She turns to the right.

This one – shows the little parting gift Davey left me.

I can say his name now and it doesn't hurt.

Davey. This is what he left behind when he walked out. Grass's slash, the girls call it. The last night I was with him, he showed me his knife. A flick knife, which he flicked over me. Payment in kind, he said. Davey.

Your daddy, Jordan.

He wasn't all bad, though. Roars into my life; me nineteen, him from Birmingham, which to us spelled glamour. He'd been exiled there by the local police. 'Yeah, I'm exiled. I'm living in exile, 'en I?' Should've given me some warning. He roars in on a big fucking motorbike. Stops right in front of me; helmet off, black hair. 'Get on,' he says. 'Who the hell d'you think you are?' 'Get on,' he says again, and I do.

He took me for a ride.

I'd already worked my way through a good number of the available men in Morecambe. I had a fast turnover; I threw them over like red rough onion skins, in my search for that pure white core, strong enough to make your eyes water. Damp alleys, backs of cars, rarely beds. Men like lard; men like soggy chip papers in the rain.

But Davey was different. With him, it was all going to be different. We were in love, he told me. It was official. 'Yeah, I love you, Shirley girl, ok? Don't expect me to keep saying it.' He brought me flowers sometimes, still wet from the gardens he'd nicked them from, and furry chocolates too. I didn't mind. You take what you can get in this world, don't you? I did. Seized this unlikely lad with all my might. I wanted him because he was different. Different spelled exciting; spelled love, spelled future, spelled take me away from here and breathe life into me.

So he took me away. He'd take me away from the little shop where I worked. Fizzy drinks, tea towels and things made out of seashells. Us roaring down the prom, strolling old ladies tutting: 'She'll come to no good!' But I didn't care! For the first time in my life I felt awake. Everything before had made me tired. I dozed through school, I slept through years, dreaming of somewhere else. 'She's not overly bright, our Shirley,' said my mum. 'But she'll find herself a man all right. No mistaking that. Ooh, she's lovely-looking.'

Thanks, Mum. Well, I kissed a hundred frogs. Mind you, Jordan, so did Mum. Married a toad. My dad. When I was a kid he seemed huge. Thick brows, pop eyes, big fists. It wasn't till I grew up that I realised what a shortarse he was. Some days my mother would appear with strange colours on her face, swollen like she'd been to the dentist. Used to frighten me, that. Cause no one else could see the colours 'cept me. Neighbours, ladies in shops, my brothers. Everyone acted like they weren't there. I used to hide from that face. Those days my dad always bought her big, yellow flowers and cards with poems. 'Roses are red, violets are blue, bruises are green but I still love you.' And she'd kiss him and make a nice pot of tea. Well, you've got to be kind to be cruel.

Compared to Davey, everything else is dull, damp. I hate the bloody sea, hate the day-trippers from Manchester and the students from Everywhere. I hate the talking video games on the prom and the never-ending bingo. I live for the times when he wraps himself around me and roars me away on his monster motorbike. I feel so alive, so unsafe.

You loved it too, that feeling, didn't you?

She mimes swinging Jordan up in the air.

I'm going to throw you away. One – two – three!

Pause.

The shrink I see in there, he says I wanted Davey to be my father. Crap, I say. I just always went for the dangerous ones. Moved towards the flame like a blind woman, drawn in, feeling the heat. I didn't want some sad fuck, did I? Or some poor sod dressed up as a hamburger, prowling round the shops. I didn't want someone as dead as me.

And Davey was really dangerous. He took me away from the rain and the tea towels and the lard, all the way down the M6 to Portsmouth! I clung tightly to his back as we made our escape. All I took with me was some knickers and my tapes.

We got a little flat together. Swirly-whirly carpets, dead flies on the windowsill and a bed that came out of the wardrobe. Seven floors up with a view.

He said we'd call our first kid Meatloaf and we both laughed . . . At nights we'd go to the pub and slag people off. We slept most of the day. I was in heaven! Me, him and the bike; our own little threesome. I wonder which one of us he preferred. The bike certainly took up all his Saturday afternoons. 'Make us a cup of tea, doll,' he'd mumble as I walked by with the shopping.

One night we got a carry-out and sat in front of the telly. He went to the bog and I took one of his beers and shook it. 'Here you are,' I said, 'Open that one.' It went all over him.

He stopped me laughing with a punch. It was the first time. I felt so stupid.

Pause.

When my periods stopped I thought it must be the drink. Not you. Not into our world. Not so soon.

When I knew, I was sick straightaway. 'I'll give you something for morning sickness,' said the doctor. He looked at me with distaste, as if he saw so many thick, careless sluts like me it made him weary. But it wasn't morning sickness. It was fear.

'Davey,' I said, 'I'm up the duff.' And I waited. But there was just this . . . silence. Then he smiled, stupid like, and he went down the pub on his own. He came back, beery and staggering, and he planted his lips on my belly. 'You silly bitch,' he said.

Next morning he disappeared and I didn't see him for two weeks. He came back brazen and sheepish, with a new tattoo and a rash. He looked at me awkwardly all the time. He packed me in drinking and smoking and he wouldn't let me ride on his bike any more. He said I disturbed the balance. As I got bigger, he made a show of listening for kicks but he was always pissed off and he spent less and less time at the flat. Strangely, I didn't care. I knew we were going to be all right. Our own little family. I was going to be part of something – I was determined! Fuck alone knows why I thought that. Must have been my hormones. I just hung around like a big placid cow, watching crap telly and enjoying the adverts. I knew all the words off by heart:

'When the dirt says hot but the label says not.' 'One fairy lasts longer than two cheapies.' 'Shampoo and conditioner? Not me.' 'Once driven, forever smitten.'

I wanted to step into the adverts, Jordan, and lead a shiny life.

Maybe I thought that despite himself, Davey would want kids. He ran away from home when he was thirteen, wouldn't say why. We knew so little about each other. I never talked, he never listened.

I grew as big as a whale wearing a tent. He hadn't touched me for weeks. One night, as I lay on the sofa listening to you move inside me, he comes in with a woman. I didn't know her; face like a rat and a frizzy perm. He must have been fucking desperate. 'Hello Shirley, love,' he says, 'This is Maureen.' I can't speak. 'Who the fuck's she?' says Maureen. Who the fuck indeed?

Who?

He puts on a record and they start to dance, as if I wasn't there. She puts her tongue in his ear. They're both pissed. 'Aren't you going to get your kit off?' says Davey. 'Where's the fucking bed?' says Maureen, and Davey opens the wardrobe.

I lie on the couch inches away, hugging you to me, listening. I can't help it.

Next morning she scurries away, leaving behind fag butts and a stain. I pretend it hasn't happened. Davey's hands become rough, they rub me raw. His mouth, slackened by drink, makes ugly shapes at me, like he's trying to say something, something lost in his eyes saying 'don't blame me'. I keep very quiet, trying to make him believe I'm not really there, in case it annoys him when I move, when you kick harder; getting nearer the world.

I'm scared of his hands. When he hits me, I think of big yellow flowers . . . And it's true about the bruises. No one else can see.

You can get used to anything. 'I'm sorry, doll,' he says, head on one side, running his fingers through his black hair. He's always sorry after.

I hated you then. I spent the last weeks sitting by the grey window looking over the roofs to the sea, like a line in the distance. The air was still and the ground was very far away. The gulls circled round and round and round. I hated the noise they made. I waited.

I waited for it to be over.

Pause.

When the queen gave birth to a perfect baby boy, there was rejoicing throughout all the land. The king was very proud of his beautiful young wife who could not only spin straw into gold but could provide a son and heir to the kingdom. The queen had meanwhile forgotten all about her promise to the strange little man who had saved her life by filling the room with gold.

She lived in blissful happiness until one day, as she was alone in the gardens with her child, she heard singing and her heart

turned to ice because she recognised the voice. She held her
child close to her breast and quickly turned back towards the
palace. And there he was, the weaver of gold, standing before
her, his beard tucked in his belt.

'I've come to claim my prize, fair queen,' he grinned. 'What do
you mean?' she cried. 'Your son,' he said. 'You must give me
your son, as you promised, your firstborn child.'

The queen was terrified, and offered the little man all the
wealth of the kingdom if he would let her keep the child. But
the mannikin said: 'No; I would rather have some living thing
than all the treasures of the world. Now give me what you
promised.' The queen began to moan and weep and threatened
to turn all the forces of the palace against him, if he did not
leave.

The little man laughed. 'Do what you will,' he said, but have no
fear, I shall take your son, even if it means spiriting him away
by magic!' The poor queen wept tears of such grief and begged
so piteously, that the mannikin at last felt mercy touch his heart.

'I will strike a bargain with you,' he said. 'You have three days
to guess my name. If you discover it, you shall keep your
child.'

Pause.

And then you came.

God, you were beautiful. A soft halo of thick black hair,
several shades darker than Davey or me. Davey takes one look
at you and says, 'He's not my kid! He's too fucking dark!'
You're so small. I'm so frightened. You seem too small to
survive. Tiny hands, clutching at air. Mouth a small rosebud,
opening to wail, my baby.

That's when I found out I was a killer. I was in the hospital.
Someone had a paper and they read a story about an evil
monster who beat his kid to death while his wife stood by and
watched. There we all were, in our padded dressing gowns and
fluffy slippers, some with babies, some still pregnant, disgusted
by this man. 'If any bastard tried to do that to one of my kids,
I'd bloody kill him,' said this woman who had five kids
already. And we all agreed. We were a band of killers with our

sore tits and sanitary towels like the seat of Davey's bike. A lethal team. And I belonged.

I never knew what loving someone was before you. When I hold you I don't want anything else at all. Davey mutters under his breath. He never looks at you and his eyes never meet mine. He says I stink of baby sick and shitty nappies. He doesn't like my stretchmarked stomach, soft and furred with the purply scars I am so proud of. He doesn't like my breasts, sagging and full of milk. I am different. I stop picking up the empty cans and the women with their stains don't bother me any more. I forget that Davey is any part of you; you are all mine. I am all yours.

I carry you round on my chest in a pouch, like an animal. Shopping bags in my hands, you sleeping or searching, eyes closed, for my breast.

I let myself into the flat, breathless from the stairs, hands raw where the bags cut into them. I catch the end of a noise, a soft, soft noise, maybe a moan. In the scrubby gloom I see a woman bent over Davey. His trousers are concertina'd at the ankles. I almost laugh. The woman still has her clothes on, stilettos snagging the carpet, greasy skirt pulled up over her hips, claggy knickers showing and her nails, clutching his thighs, are painted black. I see all these things, little things indeed; I file them away very fast, deep inside me. Davey's face is all concentration.

At last I drop the bags and their heads turn towards the noise. Davey looks at me and his eyes say 'See?' The woman swallows, gagging, and starts to pull her mouth away from him. Davey winces and you let out a wail. 'Oh, don't try to explain,' I say to this creature on the carpet. 'Weren't you ever taught it's bad manners to talk with your mouth full?'

There is a little silence, while we all wonder what to do. 'Carry on,' Davey says at last, pushing her head back down on him. 'Why don't you bite it off, love?' I say. 'I fucking would.' She spits at us both and leaves, sorting out her knickers on the way down the stairs.

I've never seen him so angry. His eyes are black like stone in water. 'Can't you shut that fucking baby up?' he yells, and he

lunges towards us, falling over his trousers and his stiff little
dick, arse in the air like a brown, hairy balloon. I laugh. I can't
stop. That's it. Next thing I feel is his fist smashing my mouth.
I taste the blood and he hits me again. I feel the jagged edge of
a broken tooth against my lip, and more blood. You are red and
howling against my chest. There's no time! I can't stop him!
The third blow comes to me softly, through your body. There is
silence then, until I start to scream. I look like a monster, blood
dripping onto my chest. I hear a voice in the distance: 'Jesus
Christ, man! What the bloody hell do you think you're doing?'
It's Nerys from downstairs, drunk and blowsy as always,
standing in the open doorway, cardie askew.

'Shall I call the police, Shirley love?' 'Sod off,' says Davey and
slams the door on her. I'm still screaming. 'You fucking grass,'
he says and he gets out his knife, quick as silver.

He moved out. We had no money, you and I, but we got by
somehow. You do, don't you? I found a way. Get on your bike
and look for jobs, the man said. So I did. Blow jobs, a fiver a
time. Trade was good and I was only doing what I did before
I met Davey; but this time it was better. I was getting paid for
it, see? I bought you clothes, and tiny toys . . . Bears with pink
ears and a little rabbit that you loved, with a bell round its
neck. You loved the sound of that bell. Wouldn't be parted
from it.

And we were happy. Your first word was sun. I used to talk to
you all the time. There was no one else to talk to, ever; and
you listened. I used to say to you, 'Look, there's the sun,
Jordan, sun! Isn't it lovely? It means that God is smiling at
you, Jordan.' 'Sun,' you said, one day, out of the blue, your fat
baby finger pointing straight at it and then you began to laugh
and laugh, and gurgle, and I cried, and held you so tightly that
you squealed with pain and surprise.

You slept with me. I was too jumpy. Every little noise and I
thought it was you suffocating, choking, dying in your cot.

We used to go and walk by the sea. Me pushing your buggy,
all wrapped up in my old jumpers, like a bag lady; you
swathed in layers of wool, and nylon and gloves and scarves,
like a round bundle of rags, chirping away to yourself. Old

ladies cackling at you and smiling at me. I couldn't talk to them. I was somewhere else, smiling back but distantly, giving a silent warning; Keep Off The Grass. We used to go down to the sea and just stare out at it. You loved the waves. I loved the noise they made, falling over and over, like breath.

I often hear that noise now. Comforts me at night.

Pause.

They left me some magazines and a drink and some yoghurt. It was nice of them; they didn't have to do that. There's a bloke next door. I know because I heard him shouting a while ago. He wanted a piss, poor bastard.

Pause.

And then Davey comes back. Different. Wearing a shirt, and someone's ironed the collar. Clean jeans. Jesus Christ, I think, and then I see why. A woman follows him in; bubbles of blonde hair piled on her head like a poodle in a show and she's plump, but smart, really smart.

'This is Barbara,' he says. 'We're getting married.'

'That's nice,' I say. 'Congratulations.' He walks all around me, circling me, round the flat, with Barbara tugging at his arm, whispering at him.

'Look at the state of you,' he says. 'You look like shit. And look at the state of this place.'

Barbara flicks some of the dirt off the table. 'D'you want a cup of tea then?' I says to her. 'I wouldn't even sit down in here!' she says, and off she goes to inspect the toilet. The bath is steaming, full of your dirty nappies.

'Been hearing about you,' says Davey. 'Been hearing about what you been up to.'

'Oh yeah?' I blink and the red behind my eyelids blurs my sight. Damned if I'm going to cry. Barbara sniffs and tugs Davey towards the cot where you lie. She picks you up. 'My God, he's beautiful!' she says. And you betray me by smiling at her. 'Barbara's a natural with kids,' says Davey, proudly. 'Oh my God, he's so beautiful!' she says. I want you to scream at her as if she's acid in your face but you start to gurgle, too generous in your love. How can you know that you are all I have?

'You're not fit to look after him,' says Davey. 'Not a slag like you.'

'She's dressed him in pink,' shrieks Barbara. 'Pink and he's a boy!'

'He needs to be taken away,' says Davey.

Taken away.

Two little words like drops of acid.

I went mad. I threw everything I could find, howling, howling like a cat. They fled, clattering and threatening all the way down the stairs. 'Whore!' shrilled Barbara. Nerys banged on the ceiling.

There were no more men after that. No more odd men; men in pubs; men who reek of beer and pies, men with lazy eyes travelling up and down, assessing the meat for plumpness, freshness, stamina. No more nights spent under these men. No more hands touching but not seeing. No more foul breath on my neck. No more hours wasted; waiting, waiting; dry lips, creased skin, legs goosepimply and cold, selling my wares. No more.

Never warmed me up, those men. Left me cold. Cold. Cold.

I used to pay a kid from the flats to sit with you while I was out. A twelve-year-old bloody kid; someone too young to know my shame. Jesus Christ! Anyone could have taken you from me then.

I'd come in blue and shaking with cold, the shape of their hands still printed on me; blank inside. I'd pay the kid and he'd bugger off. Then I'd go towards you and pick you up and you'd be warm; so warm; always warm and wriggling, giggling, my baby.

Playing with you on the sofa; a game where I hide the rabbit with the bell and you scream and laugh until you find him. I hear a tiny, gentle sound and I see that a letter, a letter in a white envelope has landed on the mat. There's typing on the front. I don't open it for hours but I can't think about anything

else. I put you down for a nap and when I read it I'm sick.
'Dear Miss Jones, My client has instructed me to begin
proceedings . . . ' and then something about 'custody' and
'unfit mother'. 'My client informs me of his fears that the
named infant is at risk in your care.' There is nothing bad
enough I can do with this letter. In the end I tear it with my
teeth into a thousand pieces and when it's no more than mush
and spit I take it to the window and throw it to the gulls.

But the letters come thick and fast. First from Social Services,
then from the council, then another white envelope with
writing saying I've been summoned. I chuck them in the bin.
When people knock at the door, I never answer. I just sit with
you in the toilet until they go away. Two ladies come and shout
through the letterbox. 'Are you all right, dear?' I stop going
out. It's too dangerous. Anyone might be waiting there.

But I know. I know they are coming. We can't hide in the toilet
for ever. I imagine them breaking the door down with axes and
grabbing you out of my arms! I imagine them ambushing me
when I go out for food! I imagine them surrounding the block
of flats and starving us out! I turn all the lights off and we
crawl about on the floor below the level of the windows. You
think it's fun.

Days pass; maybe weeks, maybe months. I don't know because
each moment seems the same; grey and small.

I wash your clothes in the bath, again and again, and when
they're all wet, I dress you in old T-shirts of mine.

Then one day we come to the end of the dry Rice Krispies and
the packet soups. I feed you the last egg, the very last egg, and
a few hours later you begin to cry with hunger.

I take you to the window and we look down. And there they
are, same as always, hundreds of them watching us, listening
to you cry. Surrounded. There they all are, shimmering, all the
ladies and the solicitor and the people from the council, and
Davey and thingy, poodle-dog, whatever her name is, and she
floats up to the window and leers in shouting: 'He's crying!
She's making him cry!'

Please don't cry. Please, don't cry. Please . . . don't cry.

I watch until it grows dark, and the people outside all fade into the shadows. Somehow, in the darkness, they seem to lose their strength. I move from the window and look all around the little flat. So small, so bare, a haven no longer. You're tired out with sobbing and while you sleep, I bundle you into your pram.

We creep past Nerys' door. I can hear her telly, loud and ordinary. The pram wheels squeak but we get away. The street is vast, veering away towards the sky, and my feet feel light as they touch the pavement. I am glad I have the pram to keep me on the ground. I can hear the sea breathing in the distance.

I know where I am going. I buy a bottle of vodka and four packets of aspirin and that's it; the end of the money. On the way back, we go down to the sea. I take you out of your pram and we watch the waves, black and silver in the darkness. So much space. We stand on the edge of the path to the moon, the diamonds on the water blinding me. So much space . . .

'Time to go,' I say. And then we go back. Walking along the shore I start to laugh. I remember that. I walk so slowly, holding you tightly to me. I leave the pram sitting on the shore; a gift for the waves. We won't be needing it any more. We'll be up there, in that space, gliding on the water to the moon . . .

Back in the flat, I turn on the lights, for the first time in . . . years! Bright, bright dazzling lights. You blink with surprise, and when I look at you, I know I'll need the drink first, because I am a coward after all. I lay you down to sleep and I drink.

She drinks.

I drink the vodka, gagging on the strength of the aspirins. Then, I can't remember. I can't remember, Jordan.

I can't.

I take up a pillow and without looking I place it over you, so so gently and I press down on it for a long time, without looking. I can't look, in case . . . I see you kick.

Then – I go into the kitchen and swallow the rest of the pills.

She drinks. She drops the bottle.

Smashes. Smashes everywhere. I think . . . I'm making a lot of noise. Then I can't remember anything else. I can't remember anything else . . . because everything else is long gone.

During the night, the queen tossed and turned, calling to mind all the names that she had ever heard. And she sent messengers all over the country to enquire, far and wide, what other names there were. When the little man came on the next day, she began with Caspar, Melchior, Balthazar and mentioned all the names which she knew, one after the other; but at every one, the little man said, 'No, that is not my name.' On the second day, she suggested to the mannikin all the most unusual and strange names. 'Perhaps your name is Cowribs, Spindleshanks or Spiderlegs?' But he answered every time, 'No, that is not my name.' By the third day, the poor queen was in despair. She pulled out her hair with anguish, trying desperately to think of every last name under the sun. She could tell the king nothing of this, because he would be so angry when he discovered that she had deceived him with her golden straw. He would surely have her killed!

As dawn was breaking, she made her decision. She took up her child and fled into the fading darkness and the king never heard of her again.

Pause.

Later, days later. I was sitting under those bright lights. It turns out Nerys called the police when she heard the bottle smash. They took me to the hospital; had me pumped out.

They told me it was the sound of breaking glass that had saved my life.

She picks up the magazine and flicks through it.

'Win a holiday in the Caribbean. It's worth over £2,000. The fine, white sand will caress your feet as you sit at the hotel breakfast table, laden with tropical fruit.'

She flicks again.

'How I Became a Wife from Hell: Reader Confidential. If you have a true experience you would like to share with other readers, your anonymity is assured and we'll pay £100.'

Oh.

She flicks again.

'Twenty wicked questions we ask Cilla Black. "Have you ever had a broken heart?" "Yes. When Elvis married I cried for days." '

Oh.

She chucks the magazine away.

It must be soon. I'll have my yoghurt.

She picks up the yoghurt.

No fucking spoon. Bollocks.

Peach Melba. Oh.

She slowly eats the yoghurt with her finger. Pause.

I loved him, you know. I loved him more than life, more than anything in the world. More than life. Sometimes, just before I'm fully awake, I think he'll be there, beside me, but he never is. Not any more.

Prison.

Jordan? For days I didn't know where I was. 'Don't tell them what you're in for,' the officer said to me when I came in. 'They'll go for you. Hate anything to do with kiddies they do, this lot.' So I said it was drugs. It helped, and I wanted so badly, so badly to believe it. I said that I imported a load of heroin. 'Oh, skag?' they said. 'Skag? No, heroin.' I said. They looked at me funny.

I put your pictures up on the pinboard above my bed. I stapled one to the pillow. I made sure you were everywhere, everywhere I turned. You smiling in your pram, you in the bath, you with the furry rabbit, you asleep, thumb curled into your mouth.

They'd put me in a dorm with three other women. Perhaps they thought the company would do me good. One of them was called Dotty, poor cow. Fancy being on the nut wing, called Dotty. 'Have you got any dog-ends for me?' she used to say all the time. 'Any dog-ends?' She'd rummage through all the bins in everyone's cells, looking for leavings. Fucking incredible, she could make a rollie out of anything, that woman.

When she saw the photos of you, she sat on my bed. 'Is that your kid then?' she says, smiling. 'Is someone going to bring him up for a visit?' Brown teeth and her face aged by drink. 'He's a lovely little fella, in' he? 'Ow old is he then?'

'Thirteen months,' I say. 'I betchyou miss 'im, dontcha? I miss my kids something awful . . . ' Then she tells me about her kids, and thankfully I don't have to talk any more. Potty fucking dog-end Dotty.

She puts her skinny arm around me when I cry.

She moves.

Your second word was Ma. Mamamamama. You said it all the time then, when you learnt how. You were so proud, pointing at me saying Ma and I'd blow kisses on your tummy.

'It's no good for you, lying there crying,' says a lady one day; big, like a box in a tweedy suit. She smells lovely, so I know she isn't from the prison. 'Come and do some art,' she says, patting my hand. So I trail after her down the corridor. We all sit painting with our fingers because brushes are too dangerous. I draw some big yellow flowers. 'Aren't they nice?' says the lady. She says she'll come and visit me once a week, if I want, but as soon as she goes away I forget who she is.

I find plenty of places to cry in the cell. I cry by the window; I cry by my bed; I cry in the tiny dark smelly toilet. When I get bored of crying in one place, I move. The tears are silent but they still get on everyone's nerves.

No difference between night and day. The others play cards wearily and write letters home, while I see a parade of passing shrinks. Tall shrinks, small shrinks, bald shrinks, old shrinks. Shrinks with glasses, shrinks with half-glasses; shrinks who smile, shrinks with mouths like cats' arses. And one shrink, my favourite, with a big wart by the side of his nose. It's all I ever look at when I'm with him.

He and I play a little game. He waits for me to speak and I wait for him. He always wins. Perhaps I know he'll have nothing interesting to say. He waits, I am waiting; it's different. 'Let's just go over it all again until I'm quite clear in my mind of your motivation,' he says, running his finger over his wart, aware that I am staring at it. So I tell him, all over again. 'Again, please,' he says, when his pen can't match my runaway words.

Fast:

I laid him down to sleep and I drank. I washed the aspirins neatly down my throat. I drank fast and furious out of the bottle, gagging at the strength of the spirit. I was nearly sick. Then – I can't remember – I can't remember! I can't. I took up a pillow and without looking I placed it over him, so so gently, and I pressed down on it for a long time, without looking. I couldn't look, in case . . . I saw him kick. Then I went into the kitchen and swallowed the rest of the pills and I drank and I drank and I drank. Then – then I dropped the bottle. Smashed everywhere. Smashed.

Each time I see them I never learn to give only the smallest crumb. I bare all and each time without fail, the pain is left, screaming bloody raw, the stale sticking plaster ripped off cruelly, without thought. No lint but acid, neat to the wound.

Maybe I never cried enough.

Now I can't hold you I'm always cold, so cold. Frozen up. I am cold even in the summer, with the heat of the sun striping my skin through the bars. I sit on the radiator by the big window and try to catch its rays. They seem to go right through my hand.

I started to cut myself to see if the blood still ran, trickling down my thin, papery skin. I thought the liquid would be blue, but it was still red and dark and alive, disappointingly.

The thing about death is, it doesn't come easy. You really have to work at it, and you have to be bloody determined; because death knows if you aren't.

I tried drinking shampoo; but it only came in little sachets and all it did was make me puke. I sawed away at my wrists, with the blunt rusty razor they gave us to shave our legs for visits. Every day an officer tipped pink disinfectant down our sink and I cupped it in my hands before it disappeared and drank it. One time I fetched a cup of boiling water secretly from the urn. I mixed four spoons of sugar in it and threw it down my neck. The pain was a relief.

Death always defeated me. Jesus wants me for a sunbeam.

The woman next door, she isn't coy like me. Oh no. She's a screamer, is Christine, and a banger and a wailer, and she has a little, round red hole, right smack in the centre of her forehead. She bangs her head, see, against the wall, the floor, the metal sink. 'It's the only way,' she says. Sometimes I feel myself burning, trembling, a shudder running through me, and I cover my eyes and swallow and it goes back from where it came. 'You should try it,' she says.

When I was a kid, sometimes Dad would pile us on to a bus and we'd go a little village by the seaside. There was a white church with old paintings that my mum used to like and a path along the cliffs. My dad would sit on the beach wearing a silly hat, trouser legs rolled up. My brothers and sister and me would run along the cliffs. I used to go for miles, playing a game where I was a spy, or a princess, running from trouble.

One day I almost ran into an old man. He was sitting there very, very still. He was wearing a jumper but he looked like a king, so I told him of the armies I was running from. He nodded and asked if I would like to sit with him for a while. He said if I kept very still, the soldiers probably wouldn't find me. He asked me if I knew who had made the cliffs, and how. I said no, I didn't. So he told me about ice, and dinosaurs, and terrible storms, and the Cracking Of The Earth. It was the best story I ever heard. When my dad came looking for me it was growing dark. He gave me a thump and put me back on the bus.

And then my mum comes to visit.

She looks round, worried she might catch a disease, from being in the same room as prostitutes, drug addicts, thieves . . . murderers. She hangs onto her bag tightly, wearing a headscarf so that no one'll recognise her, because there are bound to be plenty of people from Morecambe strolling round Holloway Prison, aren't there?

I put on a frock and some lipgloss.

'Hello, Shirley love,' she says, looking round uneasily. 'Come and sit down. People are looking.'

People aren't looking, they're wrapped around their boyfriends, snogging away, eyes closed, some tearful, some just hungry.

'There,' she says. 'That's nice, in't it?' We have a fag and she asks me how I am. 'I'm fine,' I say. 'Do they treat you well?' 'Yes,' I say, 'they treat me fine.'

I lost touch with her when I went away with Davey. She said she heard about you when the local paper phoned her for a quote or two. We sit silent and apart. I can't go back, and she can't come forward. She looks so old, so tired.

'Why didn't you come to me with him? The baby – '

'Please don't, I'll scream.'

Then she says . . . 'I'm sorry, Shirl, I'm sorry.' And her eyes fill up.

Don't be sorry, Mum, Please don't be sorry. Please, don't . . .

She asks could she come back and see me again? 'Oh yeah,' I say, 'I always like some company. It gets lonely, you know, just me and the cockroaches.' And we smile at each other.

We never talked, me and my mum. And now there's everything in the world left to say.

'I just want to know,' she says. 'Did you love him?' They have to take me away shortly after that.

My lawyer began to come more and more often. Posh. He tried to give me some chocolate once but it wasn't allowed. Kind and posh. He brought statements with him from police; forensic scientists; prison staff; and of course, psychiatrists.

'Jones presents an attitude. She is reluctant to talk, giving sly glances at me, but is unable to meet my eyes. Her manner may be manipulative; she has obviously learned to relate to men in a sexual manner and this was apparent throughout our meetings.'

Cunt.

'On talking to prison staff, I gleaned that she exhibits her remorse through bouts of tearfulness, self-mutilation and sullen silence. When asked if she regretted what she had done, she refused to answer and this indicates to me that she is trying to give the impression that she was not responsible. Jones has refused her solicitor dialogue with me, telling him that she considers psychiatrists to be a load of crap. From this, I conclude that she has a problem with authority and courts controversy. She is definitely fit to plead.'

Nerys told them about Davey hitting me. Her statement was like a Reader's Confidential; blood everywhere. Davey told them I was a common prostitute. 'I'm not the father of the kid,' he said. 'Can't be.'

Back on the wing, I took to scrubbing the floors. I didn't have to, but anything was better than waiting, lying on the bed all day. I washed the corridors of power with carbolic soap, shedding the skin of my hands on the toil. I cleaned out the bathrooms, pulling a tangle of assorted hairs out of the plugholes. I polished the tiles until they gleamed and everyone was very pleased with me. The nice lady came back and said I should get a gold star.

I even went down the gym once. There were these two big men there. Bill and fucking Ben, trying to get us to do press-ups. But we were all on too much medication and we just lay on the floor like dead fish. 'Come on, darlin',' said one of the men. 'You want to lose a bit of that flab.' He reminded me of a bloke I'd once shagged in a car park. I told him to fuck off and they took me back to the wing.

That's me, hard as nails.

Your second Christmas came and went. No presents, no visits to Santa, no nativity. Dotty made us snowmen out of sanitary towels and we all made cards in art. I sent one to my mum and she sent me one back with a candle on it.

Then it was time to go to court. There were seven of us making appearances that day. We all met in reception with our best clothes and borrowed tan tights. 'Don't look at the jury, whatever you do,' one of them told me. 'It sets them against you right from the start.'

The nice lady lent me a handbag. I had nothing much to put in it.

She takes a toy rabbit out of the bag, looks at it for a moment and quickly returns it.

But I took it anyway. It's nice, isn't it?

I never showed anything, Jordan, first day of the trial. Valium
in my veins, forensic photos of you in my head. What could I
say? I never blinked, never moved a muscle. I dug a safety pin
into my wrist so hard that tears of pain came to my eyes. I
concentrated all of me into that and of course, I looked at the
jury. 'Stand up,' someone would say, and I did.

'Shirley's no trouble at all,' they said about me. 'A model
prisoner. Wish there were more like her.'

I heard about people who laugh in the dock, who start to smile
and giggle at the most awful moment. Now I know why.

On the third day I had to go in the box. I could see the nice
lady sitting in the gallery and I smiled at her. It saved me from
looking at my mum.

The wig from the Crown, the other side, spoke to me like I was
a child; an evil lunatic.

'So, Miss Jones. You say that you left the pram on the shore?'

Yeah.

'Because you knew you wouldn't be needing it again?'

Yeah.

'So you are telling the jury that the killing was premeditated?'

No . . . I . . . you don't see . . .

'I think I do see, perfectly clearly. You intended to return
home, having purchased drugs and alcohol, and murder your
child, the victim, Jordan Jones.'

She starts furiously fast but breaks down.

I washed the aspirins neatly down my throat. I drank fast and
furious out of the bottle, gagging at the strength of the spirit. I
was nearly sick. Then – I can't remember. I can't remember . . .
I can't. I took up a pillow – and without looking I –

Hang me! Don't let me linger on like this! I wish for the death
sentence with all my soul! A picture of him from a telly in my
head to come into focus for just a moment and I want to be
there, where he is! I long for you to place a black cap on your

head and for someone to put a noose, thick and ropey, around
my neck, and for it all to be over!

Pause.

Know what the worst thing about prison is, Jordan? For me it
isn't the food, or the smell, or the screaming you hear at night
sometimes; for me, it's the visiting room. It's other people's
kids, you see . . .

I watch them all the time. Their mothers notice but I still can't
tear my eyes away. There was one little boy about two and
he'd always be running up and down the room, restless he was,
typical terrible two. He had brown skin and hair just like yours.
He ran straight up to me once and stood looking at me, like
they do. I was frozen. I had to hold myself back from touching
him. His mum called him but he didn't go.

After the visit was over, I just sat there, blank. The screws
waited for a while then they sighed and stubbed their fags out
and took me into the search room to frisk me down. They
never look you in the eye when they do that. Makes them
uncomfortable too, see, running their hands over a perfect
stranger's body. Anyway, there isn't really a Them and an Us. I
only fight with the monsters inside me, not the ones that patrol
the corridors and lock the doors because they have some
compassion. I have none.

Every time I hear . . . Every time I hear a baby cry on the wing
below me, every time I see a woman kissing her baby's head
or sucking its toes or blowing on its soft, fat stomach, my
throat sticks hard and rasping and I can't swallow. I freeze
when I hear wailing; the crying of a child tears me into tiny
pieces. I curl myself into a ball as small and tight as I can and
move away from the noise. I want to comfort that crying child.
Davey used to say to me: 'You smother that kid. You love him
too much. It's not normal.' Oh, he was right, wasn't he?

'If the victim had been under twelve months of age, my client
would have been charged with infanticide. As the victim was
just thirteen months old, she must be tried for murder. I ask to
consider how unfit the woman you see before you is to undergo
the torture of a life sentence in prison. She should be free to
walk from this court today, to pick up the pieces of her life and

one day know the joy of bearing other children . . . ' Ha.

I walk very near to the edge of the cliffs and look down. They're all worn away by the tide. 'Erosion,' said the wise old man. 'They can only take so much and then they begin to crumble.' Waves of pain pass, breaking over my head, and I wait and I hurt less, and I think maybe it gets easier with time! Then I see a downy head, or hear a gurgle, a small fat hand reaching out, and the cliffs begin to crumble.

But now it's time to go. Jordan? One thing or the other now. A life sentence or freedom.

Freedom.

The queen and her child rode by horse for many days, over mountains, through rivers and dark forests, until at last they came to a magical land where food was plenteous and the dazzling sun always shone, a land where they played in the trees and grass, and danced together on the path towards the moon. And of course, they lived happily ever after.

SHIRLEY *exits.*

Words appear on a screen:

IN MEMORY OF SHIRLEY JONES,
WHO WAS ACQUITTED OF MURDER
AND RELEASED ON PROBATION
IN THE WINTER OF 1987.

THE DAY SHE WAS RELEASED FROM COURT
SHE COMMITTED SUICIDE.

THE LOST ART OF KEEPING A SECRET

Catherine Johnson

For Huw and Myfi

Characters

STELLA
CHRISTINE

Both parts are played by the same actress.

Setting

The action mostly takes place in Cody/Robin's bedroom. There is a single bed centre-stage, covered in a duvet and pillows. When it is Cody's room, the duvet has a Bristol City cover. When it is Robin's room, the duvet is turned over to reveal Thomas the Tank Engine.

On the back wall is a picture of Cody, aged fourteen. When it is Robin's room, the picture changes to Robin, aged three, and then sixteen/seventeen.

Other areas of action, e.g. the amusement arcade, Bristol city-centre, can be indicated in a fantastic design way.

We are in Weston-super-Mare. It is now.

At the time of going to press, *The Lost Art of Keeping a Secret* had not yet been performed.

Act One

Robin's room.

Thomas the Tank Engine duvet cover. Picture of Robin.

STELLA *is on.*

STELLA. I saw it happen, but I didn't know.

You wouldn't, it was *odd*, but . . . I honestly wasn't alarmed or anything . . .

   She is thinking.

. . . God, I can see it so clearly – the whole day, all the bits I wouldn't usually remember, but because of 'that' . . .

I got up at six. Robin was crying, he'd wet the bed, but that wasn't why . . . I think he was just bored and then I had to change his sheet, change his pyjies, Thomas the Tank to Postman Pat, see, I remember everything, and my head was just *fizzing* in that tired way, mouth full of ulcers, so tired I might have smacked him, but not that day.

He didn't like his bed much, liked ours better. He never wet our bed, but to be honest, I don't think he was that crafty. I think he'd just had too much to drink and not a hundred per cent with the bladder yet. Like his dad on International Day. Y'know I watched him once, peeing in the cupboard. Harry, that is, not Robin, forty years old and he couldn't find the bathroom.

I bloody screamed my head off! He was pissing in my shoes!

I hate men when they drink too much . . .

Robin wanted a video and I wanted my bed, but there wasn't much chance of that now, so we sat and watched Thomas over and over again. That bloody tune. Over and over.

I was wearing my white dressing gown with the coffee stain on the sleeve and he was wearing his blue dressing gown with the braiding like a little old man's.

And he sat on my lap and I could feel his little boy's bony bottom and his curly-top sweaty hair under my chin and I was in love.

Music: Thomas the Tank Engine *theme.*

Lights fade on STELLA.

CHRISTINE *turns the duvet cover. It's now Bristol City.*

Cody's picture on the back wall.

Lights up.

CHRISTINE. I'm fucked. I'm – that's it with me, I'm fucking fucked.

Good, innit? I'm indestructible.

No, I totally am.

Some days I feel like Wonder Woman, I could step out on the road and get hit by this bloody gert juggernaut or summat and it would just – buckle. Me – juggernaut, no contest. That's why I don't do it . . .

I don't know when it was. Half-term? Or was it a Saturday?

I think it was a Saturday, I was hanging – just for a change.

I know Alan was there and I really wished he wasn't. I likes my routine – Friday night on the lash with the girls, stagger in steamboats, chips in bed and a gallon of squash, wake up with my knickers at the bottom of the bed and my lenses still in . . . did I do that then and all? I don't know.

But Alan *was* there, 'cos that thing about the garage. I remember that.

'Did you look in the garage?'

She smiles.

Alan's fucking face!

Hold on CHRISTINE *for a moment.*

Cody's picture changes into Robin.

STELLA *turns the duvet cover.*

STELLA. When Harry got up, we all went to the beach. I know that sounds like the height of simplicity, Harry gets up, we go to the beach, but, God, everything was such an *effort* then. And I always felt so tired . . .

But Harry gets the lie-in, 'cos he works all week, it's only fair *I* get up with Robin, but Harry likes a shag, Saturday, so if I do get up with Robin, that's all wrong too . . .

(*Sings.*) 'There are two men in my life
To one I am a mother, to the other I'm a wife . . . '

God, that ad, where did *that* come from?

(*Sings.*) 'And I give them both the best
With natural shredded sex . . . '

Ah, the old school songs come flooding back . . .

'The Dirty Germans Crossing the Line' and poor old Mr Murphy's daughter with her tight little hole – God, I was eight years old! You forget, don't you? You think kids are so innocent – childhood is so idyllic . . . it's never been like that.

She reflects.

I remember being anxious a lot . . .

But hey ho, what do you know? Saturday comes and so does Harry –

'Blow job, darling? I've just been up for hours with wet beds and Thomas the Tank and a bowl of Weetabix that was too mushy and Marmite soldiers that were 'sick' and Meg, Mog and Owl and the shopping-game, yes, every box and can in the kitchen on the floor, I spent a bloody fortune, but he's had a bath and he's back in his bed with his emergency dummy, so why don't *you* just roll over and let me suck your cock . . .?'

Harry got up and said, 'Let's all go to the beach.' Robin was asleep. I said, 'Let's not wake him up, he'll be grumpy' – really I was hoping I could sleep too then, but Harry got another hard-on so . . . I'm making it sound like I was *such* a martyr, no, to be honest, I felt sorry for the bloke, I was always so tired, so wrapped up in Robin, it was just a quick and easy way to make him feel special too . . .

But I didn't sleep and . . . I'm making excuses. I *was* tired,
that's why I didn't do anything but . . . I was tired, but I'd have
done something. If I'd known.

She says nothing for a moment, looking at us.

The Robin picture changes to Cody.

CHRISTINE *turns the cover, then sits down on the bed,
scratching her wrist.*

*She scratches for a moment, then licks her wrist and puts it
behind her back, trying to find a cool place to hold it
against.*

CHRISTINE. It's Alan's house. He lived there with Sue, before
I came on the scene. Then she fucked off, when she found out,
and I moved in. And then we had Cody and then I told Alan to
fuck off. But it's still his house. So he still thinks he can come
round when he feels like it. And I can't say no. 'Cos of Cody.
All right, I don't *have* to go to bed with the bloke. I don't love
him. But you know what it's like when you're pissed and he's
pissed and you got a kid together. You start getting all 'Oh
remember?' The first couple of times it happened, I think Alan
thought it meant we was going to get back together, but that's
not going to happen. I don't like him. No point now, anyway . . .
when he's there in the morning, I just want him to go. I make
him toast and coffee and soon he's watching the clock – pub's
open. He fucks off and I goes back to bed. I don't go for the
hair of the dog. I just sleep. That's how I know I'm not an alky
– after it happened I knew they was all watching me like that –
'Oh Christine's gonna get fucked now' . . . well, I am fucked,
but not what they reckon . . . I know I'm not an alky . . .

Alan goes 'cos of Cody. Once he knew I wouldn't have him
back and be fair, if you knew Alan, you'd see my point – he
felt funny about being in the house like that, you know, being
with me. I don't know what I felt. I think I . . . I think I didn't
think about it and like, the first time, I didn't think, oh fuck,
I got to get Alan *out* of here and anyway, Cody never knew,
but . . . Alan could be right. Could be a bit of a head-fuck –
and soon as he said it, I was like, yeh, I should've thought of that.

I hate it when that happens, it's like there's a bit of my brain missing, the bit that's got any sense. And then I'm asking myself – am I really thick or what? But . . . there's a part of me that's going, 'You're just fucking selfish.' Like, if it suits me, that's it, stop thinking . . . really fucking selfish.

She is scratching her wrist behind her back.

I'm the only one who's got the guts to say it.

CHRISTINE *goes off.*

The Promenade.

Seaside sounds: gulls, children playing, surf.

STELLA *emerges downstage, holding three '99' cornets. She licks one of the ice creams, peering short-sightedly around.*

STELLA. Where are they? I told him to wait, he knows I'm as blind as a bat – yes, I have got my contacts in, but there's too many people – oh, great, what am I supposed to do now? Stand here like a na-na, with ice cream running down my arm? I can't remember what they're wearing – oh, why didn't he wait? It's so typical, just 'cos there was a bit of a queue, he can't just stand for five minutes with Robin, they have to go off and *do* something – I think Robin had the red T-shirt on, red T-shirt and shorts, red red Robin, or was that yesterday? I don't know, I can't remember.

STELLA *stops herself. Breathes.*

Ok. Ok. They're coming back and I'll just wait here. I'll just wait here till they come back. He can't expect me to go looking for him, can he? I don't know where they've gone, he knows where I am. And anyway. If they don't come back, I'll go home and I'll see them back at home. Ok. And anyway. Of course they'll come back. Why do I always . . . ? Like being on the beach, looking for Mum and Dad on the towels. Knowing they'd left me, it was all a ruse, the day at the seaside, as soon as they'd sent me off to get water in my bucket they'd picked up their towels and the carrier bags with sandwiches and Lucozade and a flask of tea for Dad . . . and I won't cry. I won't show I'm afraid. No one will know . . .

She looks down at the cornets, running down her hands.

. . . Bloody mess. Robin won't eat it now, he hates things that
have gone all sticky . . .

STELLA *carefully carries the cornets over to the waste bin
and drops them in.*

CHRISTINE *picks up a towel and walks downstage, wiping
her hands.*

CHRISTINE. All right, I give him a wank. As you do. I don't
know, it was one of those days, we were getting on all right for
a change. He even made us a cup of coffee – yeh, I know, a
hand job for a cup of coffee, how low can you go? About down
to a Jack Russell . . . well, that didn't go down on the
statement, anyway. My statement, I mean, knowing Alan, he
had to say it . . . they always called me 'Christine', never Miss
Clarke, I never said – 'Call me Christine' . . . anyway, I bet he
never let on he's a one-minute wonder. He said 'Sorry'. Like,
why would I mind? I wasn't getting anything out of it. Let me
off a sore wrist. Had to smile a bit, mind. I knew he wasn't
getting any, whatever he said. Wouldn't have come off like
Warp Factor 95.

It was only a wank. I'm not gonna get all . . . God, we done it
enough times, anyway, when we was still together – hand job,
blow job, tit job, whatever? You know, someone seen you
nuddy every night, on your hands and knees with your arse in
their nose and it's not like – back then it was all special and
lovely, now we're not together it's a bit sick. Back then I was
still like, come on, come on; it's getting on me nerves now.

Back then I got a house and a baby out of it, now it's a cup of
coffee, well, y'know . . . it's not a big deal. I never thought. No
big deal. Well. An attitude like that can run in the family and
then what?

CHRISTINE *lights a cigarette and goes over to the waste
bin. She stands there, smoking for a moment, then grinds
out the cigarette and goes off.*

STELLA *comes on, pushing a light-weight stroller. It's got
a bright, clean seat.*

STELLA (*to Robin*). We'll get another ice cream. Ok?
Mummy *had* to throw the other ice cream away, darling, it

went all runny, you wouldn't have liked it . . . well, it's in the bin, sweety, I can't show you . . . well, I didn't really know how long Daddy was going to be, did I? Daddy didn't tell me you wanted to walk on the wall. Did you see the donkeys? Did you? Were they nice? We can go on the donkeys one day, if you want to, when you're a little bit older . . .

(*To Harry.*) No, Harry – he won't hold on, he'll be scared . . . yes, I know the man'll walk with him, but look at the state of him, I'm not trusting a halfwit with my precious son . . . well, you don't need a degree to run a donkey ride, do you? . . . it's not fucking snobbish, it's common sense . . . it isn't about that . . . no, it isn't . . . it's completely different and you know it . . . look, I wasn't in a state about him walking on the wall, I didn't like you going off . . . well, all right, but I didn't know where you'd gone . . . oh, now you're just being stupid, of course I trust you with him . . . yeh, the degree helps . . .

She laughs a little. To us:

I didn't, mind, not deep down, no one, I couldn't trust anyone to look after Robin the way I could. Even when I got it wrong and I know I did sometimes – it was all so new to me, I could never get it absolutely perfectly right – but it was me that loved him best, I'm sorry, but it was, so how could I really, deep down, trust anyone?

(*To Robin.*) We'll just walk along to the end of the pier and then we'll get another ice cream, they've got lovely ice cream at the end of the pier . . . well, I don't know if they do 99s, but they've got blackberry and coffee and walnut and pineapple yogurt with real bits of pineapple . . . no, I don't know what Daddy said, Daddy's just being silly, it's lovely ice cream and at least it isn't made of bits of pig . . .

(*To Harry.*) . . . it is . . . gelatine, it's pig's bladder . . . well, everyone knows it . . . well, of course there's gelatine in ice cream, isn't there? . . . God, why do you have to contradict everything I say? Do you want me just to bring him up on junk food?

(*To Robin.*) . . . there's no pigs, darling, Mummy was . . . no, there's no pigs at the seaside, only Daddy . . . (*She laughs at her merry quip.*)

Oh, let's go on the rides. Harry? Shall we go on the pier rides?

STELLA *folds up the buggy. She lays it on the ground.*

CHRISTINE *picks up the buggy and opens it. The seat is dirty, faded and old.*

CHRISTINE. Alan says I'm a fucking squirrel, hoarding stuff away, but squirrels save useful stuff, don't they? – nuts and all. I save crap. Cody's buggy, what's the use in that? S'pose if I got my arse in gear I could take it down the dump . . . I don't know, maybe I thought I'd get some more use of it, ha fucking ha, no chance now . . . gross, innit? Bits of old rusk where he hung on at the sides – had to hang on, it was always tipping over . . . wandering round Boots with his nappies on the back, so if I got stopped I'd be like, what nappies? Those nappies? Shit, I completely forgot . . . everyone knows kids do your head in . . .

Pushed him into a rose bush once. I didn't mean to. I just let go at the top of the hill. I wanted to see what would happen. You don't just see what'll happen with kids, do you?

You got to run in there, get in the way of the rose bush. In the way of the pricks.

That is very fucking ironic.

CHRISTINE *pushes the buggy. It rolls off quickly,* CHRISTINE *following, slowly.*

The Amusement Arcade at the end of the pier.

Music: 'Magic Carpet Ride'.

STELLA *comes on.*

STELLA. Harry took Robin on the dodgems. I said I'd watch, in case he got frightened and he had to get out of the car. They won't stop the ride. He went on the roundabout once and started crying and the man refused to even slow it down so I could get on and carry him off. I had to stand there and watch. His face all screwed up and his mouth open, coming towards me, holding out his arms, 'Mummy take me,' twisting his head around as the bus or the tractor or whatever he was on went by again. And me smiling, waving, trying to keep brave, feeling like the world's biggest let-down . . .

You put tokens in these dodgems. Don't trust the kids that run it, I suppose. So you just put in your token and your car starts up and you get three or four minutes of crashing fun.

Only I told Harry not to crash. I said Robin wouldn't like it and he might get hurt. God. I'm surprised that kid did *anything*, the way I'd go on. All I could see was the bad that could happen . . . whiplash, I think I thought. So Robin chose a car – the blue one, like Thomas – and Harry put him in the safety belt and put his arm around him so he wouldn't bump about and put in the token. The car made a sort of whiney sound and they were off . . .

The first minute, I stood there, waving. Big smile on my face for whenever they looked over. It's all right! It's lovely! I'm still here and I'm smiling and waving! See me! See you! We're all here smiling and waving! And then that started to feel a bit stupid. I sort of went outside myself and I could see me, waving and that stupid smile – it felt a bit inane, really. Why couldn't I just stand there and wait without feeling some need to validate my existence? I do this. Criticise myself for something harmless . . .

Anyway. I stopped waving and smiling and just looked. Looked at the cars, going round and round and crashing. Making that whiney sound. There were two girls, fourteen? Fifteen? Big girls with baby faces. Even with the make-up you could tell they were underage – I could, anyway, maybe boys couldn't. Maybe boys couldn't care. I was thinking about me and my friend Elaine, they just sort of reminded me . . . we kept shoeboxes filled with love-tokens – the Coke bottle 'he' drank from, the cigarette stub 'he' left in the ashtray in the caff . . . I even had a potato, but I can't remember why . . .

There was a boy, on his own, but he wasn't for those girls. They didn't want the skinny kid, the kid their age, the shabby kid. He was too pale and quiet-looking and his clothes weren't good . . .

'Mummy!' And I had to look away and wave and smile at Robin again and be a good mummy . . . and now there's only a minute left . . .

They came up behind me. I felt them pass and then they were in front of me, getting into a car. It should have been a black car, but I don't know, I don't remember now. I remember the men though. Two of them. One tall and thin with dark, greasy hair in a Harrington jacket and dirty jeans. Under the jacket, his arm was in a sling. He sat in the passenger seat. The driver was older. Ginger hair. They both looked too old for the dodgems. They didn't look as if they were having fun.

I watched them. They were out of place, they didn't belong – I watched. The man with the sling pointed and the driver drove away. I looked for the girls. I knew they were following the girls. I was nosey, yes, I didn't get out enough. The girls passed, shrieking and laughing and I looked for the men, following. And then I saw the boy. Cody.

He was coming my way and the men were behind him and now I could see what they were doing, the pointing, the target – and the looks on their faces, I nearly called out –

And they hit him. Crashed into the back of his car. They were smiling. He turned.

And I was absolutely fascinated now and how much I saw and how much I imagined . . .

But the smiles I saw. And I couldn't see his face when he turned, but I saw the boy drive away and he was just – the same. Too pale and quiet-looking. No laughter. No anger. No fear.

'Mummy!' The ride was over and Robin was running from the car and Harry behind him, trying to stop him from running into the still-moving cars and me, too, coming over the barrier to catch him and whisk him up to safety . . .

I strapped Robin into the buggy. He'd loved the ride. Harry was smiling and I felt a pang of – I don't let them do enough things together . . . I looked back at the dodgem cars.

They had gone. The men had gone and the boy had gone. Cody. I looked at the people around us, they had to be there, somewhere, in the crowd, but . . . I looked beyond the dodgems and all I could see was the sky.

Lights down on STELLA.

Lights up on CHRISTINE *on the bed.*

CHRISTINE *is curled up on the bed with the telephone beside her. She is watching the telephone.*

She waits. She sits there, huddled into herself, waiting for the phone to ring.

She lights a cigarette. She smokes the cigarette down and waits.

Lights down on CHRISTINE, *waiting.*

Lights up.

CHRISTINE *is still on the bed.*

CHRISTINE. Alan kept his dope in the garage. After we split up, I mean he couldn't have kept it there before, might've got busted. He left his old bike in there and all, so if anybody asked he could say that's what he was always going in and out for. He didn't punt a lot. Bits here and there, beer money. He's not a big-time dealer. But it's enough, y'know? Too much for 'personals'. He'd be fucked if he got nicked with it and then when the policeman said, 'Have you looked in the garage?' . . . His fucking face. I'd have laughed, but . . .

And then we ran – I ran and he ran and it wasn't just the dope, it was the – hope . . .

Course he wasn't in the garage. Cody wasn't. What would he be doing in the fucking garage?

Alan made me call the police. I didn't want to . . . I didn't want to think . . . Look – he went out when we were having our coffee and messing around upstairs. I don't know when. And when I say messing around, nothing like that, well, only the hand job, but that's not like – he wouldn't have heard . . . what I'm getting at is, there was nothing – nothing – he'd have heard and got upset about, it was nothing, he just come down and had a bowl of Start and he watched a bit of telly and he went out. The telly was still on and the bowl was on the floor. And Alan went, 'What's the time?' and freaked a bit 'cos he had to meet someone down the pub and he was late, like, he sooo wasn't a big-time dealer but you'd've thought he'd get his legs broke if he wasn't on his bar stool by eleven. He had to make some calls then and I picked up Cody's bowl and there were bits of Start around the side, sticky and soggy, and I had to pick them off with my fingernails as I ran the bowl under the tap . . . I didn't know . . .

They called me Christine. And Alan, fuck me, they practically slapped his back – 'All right, Alan, how's it going?' . . . taking the piss. I didn't know them but I'm like, Alan's missis, y'know, Christine, Alan the druggy's missis, I thought they were taking the fucking piss anyway, I thought they thought – and *I* thought, *I* thought it too – he'll be back any minute, that kid, Alan's kid, Alan the fucking druggy's kid, he'll be back . . .

CHRISTINE *stares at us. Then laughs, mirthlessly. She knows we know.*

STELLA *turns the cover. The picture of Cody becomes Robin.*

STELLA *produces something from behind her back.*

It is a pregnancy test. The indicator line hasn't gone blue yet.

STELLA. I'm in the shit, a bit. There was something on the news about that boy. The local news. There was a picture, a photo from his school. He looked younger, he was smiling, I didn't see him smiling. It was him, though. They said he had been missing for a week.

I bet I went white. I don't know what that looks like, but I felt it. White and cold. If Harry had been there, I'd have said something, but he wasn't and I've got this to do now, anyway . . .

She checks the indicator line.

I'll ring when I've got Robin to bed. It's going to be a bit complicated. I'm going to have to explain why I didn't say anything a week ago, when it happened – and I'm going to look really stupid when I say I didn't know anything *had* happened . . . oh fuck. I always thought I'd be really good in an emergency, you know when you read about something in the paper, someone's been attacked and there's an appeal for witnesses, there's something about all the people who just passed by? I have a little fantasy about that sometimes, y'know, *I* wade in when everyone else is just standing there, fight off the assailants, save someone's life? (*Jolted.*) No – fuck – no, he's not . . . there'd be a body, no . . .

I didn't know. There's been nothing all week, how the fuck was I supposed to know – and anyway, what did I see, anyway? I saw him on the dodgems, that's all – he didn't leave with those men, they weren't threatening him or anything, I saw his face, he wasn't scared. All I'm going to do is witter on like a bored housewife with an overactive imagination, fuck it, I *am* a bored housewife, bla, bla . . . it doesn't matter, I have to say, it's not up to me, I have to say . . .

She checks the indicator line. It's gone blue.

Oh fuck.

The Cody picture comes up quickly.

CHRISTINE *wraps herself in the Bristol City duvet, clutching the pregnancy test in her fist.*

CHRISTINE. You cunt, you bastard, you little fucking cunt, come home, come home, come home, just –

I can't stand this, I don't want it, I want it like it was, normal, I don't know why you're doing this, I don't know what I've done . . . it's not like I had a go at you, is it? It's not like I said summat when I found out what – no, I don't know, I don't know, I don't . . . I can't go on like this, you don't know how much it fucking hurts, I wish you knew, but so what? I don't think you fucking care, anyway, you'll do what you want, you're just like your dad, oh please come home, please come home, please please please come home . . .

A telephone rings.

CHRISTINE *picks it up.*

Hello? . . . Hello? . . . Cody?

She listens, then slowly puts the phone down.

Turning away from us. She lets the cover fall, the Thomas the Tank Engine side. Robin's picture.

STELLA *turns towards us, her hand on the telephone receiver.*

STELLA. Oh Jesus, that was such a bad idea, why did I, why did I . . .? Oh God, she said 'Cody', she said his name, oh

God, why did I *do* that? I must be fucking mental, it's the baby, I know it is, it's making me mental, God, if anyone *knew* . . .

STELLA *walks towards us.*

I didn't ring the police that night. The night I heard it on the news. Robin was having one of those nights, he wouldn't go to bed, he was being a bit clingy, really – and I'd just had a shock, the test, I mean, the pregnancy test – well, I didn't mind him just sitting on my lap while we watched the telly and I thought about it all. Because. I didn't know if I wanted to get pregnant. It wasn't planned. And then I was and really there was no choice about it, because it had always been there, in the back of my mind, that Robin should have a brother or sister one day. So he wouldn't be lonely. And now it had happened and I really wanted to cry because nothing would ever be the same again. It would never be just Robin and me.

So by the next day there were two things I hadn't done. I hadn't told anyone I was pregnant and I hadn't called the police.

Look. It's not like I set out to keep secrets. And I don't tell lies. It's the sin of omission, I suppose. It's not what I say, it's what I don't say. I don't know why. It's not like I'm not saying to myself – go on then, just pick up the phone, it's simple, do it, pick up the phone, but . . . can apathy be like a mental illness? Oh, it's not apathy, it's fear – I know, I'm afraid I'll look stupid, afraid I'll get told off, afraid I'll be humiliated – I'm not happy, I'm not well, I can't cope with that right now, I can't be told it's imaginings, I can't be told it's all in my head . . .

It didn't look like him, anyway. The next day there was a photo in the local paper, the one they'd used on the news and now I came to look at it closely, I could see it wasn't him anyway. Typical me. Putting two and two together and making four million. Besides. He was older than I thought he'd be, fourteen. Skived off school a lot. This kid – not my boy, I could see that now, it really wasn't my boy – he'd run away, hadn't he? I knew where he lived, I knew that estate. He'd probably just run away.

Harry guessed about the baby. Just the next day, he said, 'Are you sure you're not pregnant?' Which is just the way he says things, we hadn't been discussing it at all. Or maybe I'd said – I don't know, my period's a bit late, or something – not then, that morning, but a couple of weeks before – something that could float around in the air and not be picked up on either way, until . . .

Because he does it too. Not saying things, I mean. I expect a lot of people do. Like not wanting to be the first to put your hand up in class, even if you know the answer.

It's easier if someone guesses what you're thinking.

So when he said that – 'Are you sure you're not pregnant?', it was easy to say, 'No, I am, actually.'

I had an idea. I showed him the photo, as if I'd only just noticed it and I said, 'Doesn't that look like the boy who was on the dodgems last week?' He didn't remember. I said he probably didn't remember because he was concentrating on the driving and Robin, but I was sure I'd seen this boy and . . .

He was giving me a knowing look. I don't know if I went red, but it felt like it. Red and ashamed. Stupid foolish woman, making things up. Making things more interesting. I saw this boy who ran away. I saw this boy who looked like this boy who ran away. I saw aliens, fairies at the bottom of the garden. I shall keep my fucking mouth shut in the future. I won't see anything any more.

Lights down on STELLA.

STELLA *goes off.*

Jukebox music – 'Nothing Compares 2 U' sung by Sinead O'Connor.

The pub.

CHRISTINE *comes on, holding a glass of brandy and Coke, a cigarette in her other hand. She is singing along to the song, swaying slightly to the music.*

She raises her glass in a gesture that is more 'keep away' than a toast. She speaks to someone in the pub.

CHRISTINE. Yeh. I'm ok. Yeh. Bearing up. Y'know. What else do you do? Yeh . . . yeh . . . yeh . . .

(*To us.*) I'm gonna stop drinking. Does your fucking head in. You let stuff in if you don't watch it. Or you let stuff out.

I know something you don't know. I know something you don't know.

(*To herself.*) Keep your fucking mouth shut and they'll go away.

(*To us.*) He'll come home. You go away. He'll come home if you go away, all right?

(*She looks around.*) I wish I could tell him. Don't come back yet, they'll ask questions. I'm trying to put the thought in his head. Like we used to be psychic? Had the same dreams? It's really fucking weird I don't know where he's sleeping . . .

I had to say about the skiving. School would've. It's not a big deal. Not like they make it sound in the papers, like he's fucking naughty – I hate that, you should see him, he's no problem. When he has the day off, we just has a lie-in and watch telly. Or he'll come round the shops with me, which I like, 'cos we don't do that a lot any more. It's like, when he was little, he'd drive me up the fucking wall in Asda and I'd be 'Can't wait till he starts school,' but now I'm pushing the trolley round, thinking how sweet he was. Always trying to be helping. (*She smiles.*) Fucking stubborn, mind. I mean, I wouldn't really have those days back, too much fucking fighting – you can't do this, no, you can't, you can't, I say you can't . . . you can't blame anyone giving up telling their kids what to do. You don't have kids to fight with. You have kids to love.

> CHRISTINE *goes over to the phone and hunkers down beside it. She watches the phone.*
>
> *Lights go down slowly on* CHRISTINE.
>
> *In the darkness, the phone rings once.*
>
> *Music – Intro. 'I Wish It Could Be Christmas Every Day' by Wizzard.*
>
> *The Cody picture changes to Robin.*
>
> *Lights up on* STELLA, *her hand on the phone. She is in semi-darkness.*

Fade Wizzard.

STELLA. I've only done it twice, I swear to God – I had a bad dream and I got scared. It's like me sleepwalking or something . . .

Shit. I hit Robin today. Right, that's a fucking lie for a start. I kicked him. I pushed him to the floor and I kicked him. A lot. I'm so tired. I've got all these presents to wrap and I've got to sort out the food and I'm so tired, I'm not sleeping, the baby's kicking all night and I asked him, I begged him to let me sleep, just an hour, this afternoon, that's all I wanted, an hour. And he kept coming in and out and shouting and laughing at me. Taking the piss, you know? I mean, he's three years old and he's calling me names and laughing and I can't take it – I don't think it's fair – and I'm out of that bed, I'm rancid with lack of sleep, and he's ran into the living room, laughing and all the presents all over the floor, all the presents I've been wrapping, he's ripped them open and they're out on the floor, his little presents I chose and hid so carefully and now I will have to do it ALL OVER AGAIN . . .

Oh please God, don't let him remember, please don't let him ever remember . . .

I only let the phone ring once. She won't have heard. I had this dream and I woke up with her number in my head and I can't think why 'cos I only called her once before. And that was months ago. Because I had this idea I could ring her. Not go to the police and everyone. Because it wasn't in the papers any more and no one seemed to be interested any more. And I knew what Harry would think if I went to the police. And I knew what the police would think of me. And if I'd tried to do it anonymously, they may have traced me. So I'd call her. And I'd just say what I saw. In case she wanted to know. And it seemed like quite a good idea, but . . . she said 'Cody'. She sounded so – scared and pleased and hopeful . . . fuck, fuck, fuck, of course she wanted to know. Of course she did.

I had a bit of a bad time after that.

He might have come home by now. It's Christmas. I think that's all I wanted to know. Has he come home yet?

I'm so tired. They keep blurring, the boy on the dodgem and the boy who ran away. And Robin's in there somewhere too and he mustn't be.

I can start again. What I did . . . it won't happen again.

End of Act One.

Act Two

Lights up on the Missing Children. On the back wall, where the pictures of Cody and Robin are, we see a slideshow of images of children who have gone missing over the years, children who have never been found. Faded school photos and family snaps. Children smiling for the camera, or looking studiously serious for a posed portrait.

This lasts for several minutes and finishes with the picture of Cody.

CHRISTINE *comes on. She stands in front of the picture of Cody.*

CHRISTINE. Thing is, it was different then. The papers didn't get so interested, you didn't get the telly round. Like now it's like it really matters, it's the headlines and there's so many pictures you're thinking you know the girl? You start to recognise her. It's always a her – I'm trying to think . . . no, I can't remember any boys. And the thing is, you know boys go too, there's always boys begging somewhere – Tescos, Barclays Bank – well, are they going home for their tea every day? Everyone thinks boys can look after theirself . . . which is really fucking screwy 'cos they can't do fuck all for theirself. I never stopped picking Cody's clothes off the floor, he'd be all 'Don't come in my room' and I'd like leave it a week but the smell'd always get me. And yeh, all right, I'd have a poke around, but he never knew – I put everything back . . .

I never bothered much with boys begging in Weston. He's not going to show up on his own doorstep, is he? I mean, I looked, but really I thought he might show up in Bristol.

I'd go in at the weekend, look around Broadmead? Course, Alan bloody wants to come and all, so he's there, trying to be all matey with these kiddies, fucking buying and selling them gear, I was a bit relieved when he topped his-self. He writes this fucking letter – 'Now my boy can come home' – fucking sanctimonious self-obsessed cunt. He was doing a lot of speed and he's crap on speed, gets these nasty bastard downers, yeh, put that in the fucking letter, Alan, it's not grief that killed you, it was Billy fucking Whizz. Twat. I don't blame Cody not coming back after that.

CHRISTINE *goes off.*

The ringing of a school bell.

STELLA *comes on, with a boy's coat over her arm.*

STELLA. I had no bloody idea she was here. I don't know if it said in the papers what she did, I don't think so, it was just her name – Christine Clarke and her age, 32, which I noticed, of course, 'cos it's my age, too. And I remember thinking we're the same age, but she's got a fourteen-year-old and mine is three. So then I supposed it was an unplanned pregnancy, because you don't plan to have kids at 18, do you? I had an abortion when I was 18 and I can honestly say I haven't regretted it once. It wasn't Harry's. I asked him once how he'd have felt if I'd had a child when he met me and he said he'd have run a mile, which is either typical of what he thinks is a funny remark or something very revealing, I don't bloody know.

So she'll be 35 now.

And the other thing I knew about her from the papers is she wasn't married to Cody's dad, because he had a different name. In fact, I don't think they even lived together, because do I remember reading he was her estranged partner? He killed himself. Poor guy. You think, Jesus, how much shit has she got to bear? Even if he was her 'estranged partner'. You see her in your mind, sort of crumpled and too thin, bad perm, she doesn't look after herself, cardies and bare legs, see her on the pier, muttering to herself. And I'm thinking, thank God I didn't speak to her, that time I was a bit all over the place, hormonal stuff, because you'd never get rid of someone like that . . .

She's not like that. She's – normal. You wouldn't know.

She's the dinner lady and she does the after-school football.
It's mixed – boys and girls, but Robin doesn't reckon girls can
play football. He doesn't seem to mind Christine, but they
haven't got any men here, anyway . . .

I cried my eyes out his first day.

Sally told me who she was. She's the first mum I've really
spoken to and I've been coming here for two years now,
dropping Robin off in the morning and picking him up in the
afternoon. I know mums to say hello to and I've had their little
boys home to tea, but it's never been anything more than 'Oh
yes, it was lovely to have him,' even if he's been an absolute
sod and Robin's begged me to make the kid go. He doesn't
really do 'socials' does our Robin. Kids his age bore him stiff,
he's much better with adults.

Sally's eldest went here, she was in the same year as Cody.
That's when Christine started doing the dinners, when he was
little. I sort of think that must be terrible, coming here every
day where her son used to be, but I suppose if she needs the
money and it's what she's used to . . .

You wouldn't think. I've seen her a bit in the playground,
when Robin's been poorly at dinner-time and I've had to come
and bring him home and she's always been very sweet with
him and said, 'See you tomorrow, Robin.' And now he's started
the football I see her Tuesdays and Thursdays after school and
we've had the odd 'How's he getting on?' sort of exchange . . .
I haven't seen her since Sally told me who she is.

Sally says everyone knows he ran away. Apparently the dad
was into drugs and Sally's daughter reckons Cody was too.
That's so sad, though I've got to say there's no way I'd let
Harry anywhere *near* Robin and Rosie if he was a junkie.
Sally says he's probably living in a squat somewhere, sticking
needles in his arm and I'm thinking '*Daily Mail* reader', but at
least she speaks to me. She says we must come round for a
meal, but I don't think Harry would ever agree.

I don't know what I'm going to say to her. Christine, I mean.
Sally says no one talks about Cody any more, it's like
everyone thinks he'll just turn up again one day and that'll be

that, she thinks it's what Christine thinks too. Because I must say she seems cheerful enough. And . . . the only thing is, I do think it's a bit of a funny thing to do. Be around kids when your own one has run away. I said this to Sally and she agreed.

STELLA *puts the coat down.*

CHRISTINE *ties a red P.E. vest on and takes out a whistle. She gets up on the bed and runs up and down, coaching.*

CHRISTINE. Come on, Aaron, run with it . . . faster . . . oh, nice tackle, Cara . . . Aaron, get up, she hasn't broke your leg . . . no she hasn't, don't be a spaz . . . Robin, are you in this game? Well, concentrate matey . . . nice pass, Jess . . .

She blows her whistle.

. . . Throw-in to the blues . . .

A beat, then she blows her whistle again.

. . . Go for it, then, come on, someone, mark him . . . Robin – buck your bloody ideas up or you're going over my knee . . .

She stops. To us:

I don't fucking believe this. I've just had Mrs Hall chewing my bloody ear off for swearing at the kids – 'I never fucking swear at the fucking little cunts,' I said.

No, I never. I just let her go on till she noticed I wasn't saying nothing? And then she gets all, 'Well, let's have your side of the story, Christine' and 'I'm really sorry about this, Christine' as if I could give a fuck. So, 'somebody's' mummy got all upset 'cos I used language, threatened him and all, yeh?, can't say who, confidentiality – like, I can't work it out? I'd wondered why she'd started coming along to watch, the other mums don't bother. Silly me, I thought she might be working up the courage to ask if she could help out, but no, she's the 'Don't let darling diddums out of my sight' type. Or the nasty, mean old world'll get him . . .

She stops. She looks agitated.

. . . Bitch. Fucking bitch. She's not a better mum – she isn't!

Hold on CHRISTINE. *Then she unties her P.E. vest and takes it off.*

STELLA *turns the vest inside out and puts it on – it's blue.*

STELLA *begins a succession of pre-match warm-ups in front of the teams – star-jumps, spotty-dogs, hamstring stretches.*

At the same time she is la-la-ing the Match of the Day *theme.*

As she comes to the end of her exertions, she applauds, enthusiastically.

STELLA. That was fan-tas-tic! You are THE BEST!

(*To us – holding her side and a little breathless.*) Yes, I know, I need my bloody head read, but it's nice for Robin I can be involved . . . and Rosie just plays in the grass or has a little sleep in her buggy . . . I mean, I hope Christine doesn't think I'm invading her territory – we haven't really talked about it, but I thought she could do with some help. She seems to get a bit stressed with the kids – and when I mentioned it to Mrs Hall, she thought it was a great idea, but I'd hate to put anyone's nose out of joint . . . it isn't that she's funny with me, she's just – a bit like I'm not in her orbit . . . I don't know – I'm positive Mrs Hall hasn't said anything and it's not like I made a big deal, I didn't want to get her into trouble, just . . .

It's weird when they're at school all day, there's these great swathes of Robin's time I don't know anything about – you go from being there 24/7 doing everything for them to just being on the sidelines a bit. I mean, I know there comes a time when you're not the most important person in their lives any more, but he's still only little and no one's going to look out for him like I do . . .

In a lot of ways, it's easier now Harry's gone. Now it's just the three of us. I'm more in their rhythm – like we have tea about four – go to bed early . . . I just eat what they do now, just sandwiches some days – and lots of nights we're all in bed together, watching a video or something – I fall asleep before they do . . .

I just want to wrap them up in a big, warm blanket and keep them safe for ever. That's the only thing that makes me sad about Harry. I really, really wanted the best for my children

and I hate it they've had to go through all this crap . . . Robin
gets angry with me sometimes and I know I shouldn't say
anything, but it's hard not to want to defend yourself and he's
always been so grown-up for his age – I suppose I do confide
in him a bit . . . I know he takes it out on me because he feels
secure in my love and he won't say anything to Harry because
Harry's the one who went away, but, you know, is that really
fair? I think I should be able to say what happened, I don't
want my son growing up thinking women should just put up
and shut up, you know, that's the way I was brought up, but
bollocks to that, I *talk* to my kids.

Beat.

STELLA *goes off.*

Bristol – Broadmead Shopping Centre.

STELLA *comes back on, wearing a coat and carrying a
couple of carrier bags from Mothercare and Marks and
Spencers. She stops.*

STELLA. Harry's got the kids today, so I've nipped into
Bristol to get their summer togs. It's easier without them. I'd
have got their shoes too, but they have to be measured, and
that's a bloody nightmare, I ought to let Harry do it really, but
he'll go getting them lace-ups when they need Velcro, he says
it's the only way they'll learn, but he's not getting them bloody
dressed every morning . . .

She stops and stares.

. . . Isn't that Christine? What's she doing here? (*Moving
away.*) I don't want her to see me, I don't know why . . . she
scares me a bit . . .

She looks back.

. . . I shouldn't just . . . she's stopped to talk to that beggar,
that's sweet of her, you'd think she wasn't the type – ugh, not
too judgmental then, what, only the lovely liberal middle
classes have got time for the homeless? . . . Oh, she knows
him, that's funny, how'd she . . . ? And he's only a kid, it's so
crap . . . oh. Oh, he . . . he can't. He can't be . . . oh my God.
Oh my God! Oh how fucking, fucking marvellous!

Lights down on STELLA.

Lights up, dimly – it is night-time.

STELLA, *sitting in the dark, in her dressing gown.*

STELLA. Can't sleep. It's always the same when the kids aren't here, it's like there's this big thing I've forgotten to do . . . and every time I hear a car, I think it's the police coming to tell me something terrible's happened . . .

I can't stop thinking about today. I'd sort of buried it, you know, it wasn't that I'd forgotten about what happened, just other stuff always overlays it, new stuff to worry about . . . God, it's like the floodgates have opened – I was shaking all the way home, I can't relax, I can't stop thinking . . .

I really, really want to know. It was him, wasn't it? I mean, I can't believe – it is just about the most fantastic coincidence in the world that I was there when she lost him and I was there when she found him again – I mean, something like that, that's got to mean something . . .

I want to tell her. I can't rest till . . . my stomach's leaping around and my head's so tight – I tried taking a couple of Nytol, but every time I think I'm going to drift off, I just snap awake again . . .

I keep thinking about ringing. It's not that late. God, maybe *he'll* answer the phone. I'll crap myself if he does.

Sometimes I feel like I haven't had a proper night's sleep since it happened. I know that's bollocks. But what if something's just there, worrying away at you? The thing you forgot to say, the thing you forgot to do . . .

(*To herself, accusing.*) You didn't forget though, did you? You *chose* not to say. You had your little secret and you kept it to yourself.

I'm going to ring. Because it's all right now . . .

Beat. The telephone starts to ring. It goes on for a while, then:

CHRISTINE. Yeh?

STELLA. I asked her if he was there.

CHRISTINE. What?

STELLA. I'm sorry, I saw you – I saw you today, is he back now? Cody? Is he home?

There's a long silence.

She didn't say anything for ages. It was very weird. I was just listening to her listening to me and then she told me. Cody wasn't there.

Oh, I'd got it all fucking wrong. That boy – that boy who'd kissed her – God, it's horrible really. She picks them up. She just started telling me – I don't know why, but it felt like she was angry – not what she said, but in her voice, it was like I'd really pissed her off about Cody and she was going to make me feel small . . .

So, yes, she fucks the homeless. Somebody's got to, she says. And look, I can see why – psychologically – her boy's run away and she's looking for him. And every time she fucks one of these little strangers, it's like she's bringing him back. In a way. But I don't know if she understands that's what she's doing. She said 'Did you think he was my son when he put his tongue in my gob?', which, of course, I *hadn't* seen and then she said 'Is that what you do with your little boy?' and I went a bit dizzy because then I realised she knew it was me.

He was upstairs. The beggar. He was in her bed. I couldn't help wondering if she made them have a wash first. And – I know she was trying to shock me and, well, I was a bit shocked, to be honest, but I still felt sorry for her. I could see it was just some desperate cry for help. And I should have put the phone down then . . .

CHRISTINE. She said, 'I know what happened to your son.'

STELLA. I've done this in my head. Over and over. The times I'd be sitting, watching telly and I'd be saying it all out in my head, saying 'Just do it. All right, it may not be the same boy, it doesn't matter, how would you feel if it was Robin? Wouldn't you want to hear something, anything?'

I even had her on my sodding 'to do' list.

And I don't know why I never called, but here she is and it's the middle of the night and she can't see me and I'm scared and I miss my babies . . .

I know what happened to your son.

CHRISTINE. And then I knew it was all over, like a little last gasp of air and it's like summat you've never talked about, never before and it's been said before you've even said it, all that's left is hearing it out loud . . .

I'm such a stupid fucking bitch. I really thought she *knew*.

I told her.

Lights slowly up on CHRISTINE.

She is kneeling on the floor, groping about under the bed.

I was looking for his socks, it's like the Bermuda Triangle in his room, two socks go in, but only one comes out . . .

She emerges, three well-thumbed porn magazines in her hands. She looks a bit amused, a bit unsettled.

She turns the pages as she continues:

Well, at least he's not gay . . .

She stops. She flicks through the pages, puts the magazine down, flicks through another magazine, quickly. She's noticed something. To us:

He'd cut out all the cunts.

She shows a page. A naked pin-up, with a gaping hole where her gaping hole ought to be.

I thought, that's fucking odd. It upset me a bit, to be honest – I mean, yeh, porn (*She pulls a face.*) – but they all do it . . . but this? (*She puts the magazine down.*) What's all that about? (*She pushes the magazines back under the bed.*)

I don't know. I never asked.

I started having a nose then. Just, you know, wondering? What's on his mind? You sort of realise you don't talk any more – just 'Have a nice time' when he goes out and 'Did you have a nice time?' when he gets back – but it's fine. We potch along. He never give me a hard time – fucking easiest kid in the world.

She lifts the mattress and starts to search underneath.

When we bought this bed, the bloke in the shop said you got to turn the mattress every six weeks. Alan said 'Fuck that for daft beggars' . . .

She brings out a crumpled pair of boys' Y-fronts.

I thought he'd shat his kecks. Hid 'em so I wouldn't go mad. But they was all bloody. It was dry and it looked quite old. But it was definitely blood.

She sits down on the bed, puts her hand under the pillow.

She brings out a wad of notes.

He had fifty fucking quid here. Fifty! And the first thing I thought was Alan's such a cunt, he's got Cody hiding his stash money and I'm sitting there with his bloody kecks in one hand and fifty quid in the other . . .

I put it back.

I wasn't gonna tell Alan, he'd have gone mad, he'd have hurt Cody – and anyway, what he did – what we both did, was fuck all to do with Alan now. I'm thinking – it's Cody's life. He's got a right to his privacy. And then, when I'm thinking we'll keep this a secret from his dad, I'm realising it's supposed to be a secret from me.

You don't have kids to rule over them. I'm not like 'You do what I tell you, I know best.'

And yeh, all right, I know some of it's down to lazy. You don't want to be always having a go, you want it to be nice? And it's like, soon as I say 'What's all this about, Cody?' – it's not gonna be nice. He's got this stuff he don't want me to know and now I know it and I'm looking at it from my point of view and, y'know, judging? And fuck it, I'm thinking, it'll all blow over anyway, I mean, I done stuff I don't go on about . . . but the bottom line is and I know this now, I live with this every fucking day – the bottom line is it was just too much fucking easier for me to pretend nothing's happened – I thought that's what he wanted . . .

I kept checking. The money went, then there was more money and then that went and then . . . I was up here before the police came round. Clearing everything out. There wasn't any money, but I took the magazines and I took his kecks . . . I already knew I wasn't gonna say . . . I didn't want them to think bad of him – I didn't want them to think bad of me. 'Cos it didn't all blow over. He went away.

Sometimes I'm hoping he's got someone who loves him. Like, he hasn't run away from home – he is home, his own home. That's summat to hang onto, but it never fucking lasts, it's always like, I never looked out for him. So he went away. I never stopped the bad things that happened, never fucking saw the bad things – in his head, in his life, I don't know. 'Cos I never thought I owned him, but it didn't mean I didn't care. That's what I want to tell him now. I do care.

Fade – Cody picture.

Fade up – Robin picture. He is now seventeen.

STELLA *is stripping the bed.*

STELLA. I never saw her after that night. She didn't come back to the school. Maybe she thought I would tell someone, but I didn't. And I didn't tell her about the dodgems. Maybe it wasn't him, anyway. It didn't really matter any more.

I don't know why she told me all that. In the middle of the night. Maybe she just didn't want to hold on to it any more, maybe it was that moment, we both felt, I don't want to keep this secret any more.

She starts to take off the duvet cover.

Well, I stopped feeling guilty after that. I did still feel sort of sorry for her, but I knew what I'd seen wasn't an innocent kid being stalked in an amusement arcade, but some kind of bizarre courting ritual. He wasn't the victim. He was calculating. Yes, he probably went off with those men, or some other men, any men, for what he could get out of them. He made me feel sick. I was angry with him. He was a little monster, he was all those little fuckers who run wild and lawless and don't care any more. I didn't think 'He was only fourteen.' I've stopped being soft. There's something very wrong and I don't want it in my world and most of all, I don't want it in my kids' world.

STELLA *exits with the bedding.*

Fade – Robin picture.

Fade up – Cody picture.

CHRISTINE *comes in with a newspaper. She rolls back the duvet. She puts the stripped pillows on top and sits down on the mattress. A doorbell rings.*

CHRISTINE *gets up and exits.*

STELLA *comes on. She stops in the doorway.*

STELLA (*to* CHRISTINE). I didn't know if you still lived here. I'm sorry, this is weird, I know, just coming round like this – but it's got beyond anything I can deal with now, I've been taking Prozac, but that didn't help, and there's no one I can talk to, no one understands . . . Robin's gone. You remember my Robin, the little boy with the curly hair? I don't know if you'd recognise him now, he's so tall and his hair's got a lot darker . . . though maybe that's just dirt, teenagers, you know . . .

I always said, we can talk about anything, I always said, I will never be angry with you, I will never turn against you . . . I thought we'd be friends. My big boy and his mum. Like equals, really, having fun . . . funny I didn't think he might turn against me, funny I didn't see that all that love was so one-sided . . . and I wasn't trying to own him, I wasn't trying to get into his head and live there, like he said . . .

Have you seen him? I've got his photo here, I thought maybe you might have seen him, or one of your friends might know him? I don't know if you've still got friends, um, who might be living like Robin's living . . . I want him to come home, Christine. I want him to come home . . .

She stops. To us:

Christine showed me the newspaper. Cody's body had been found. His little fourteen-year-old body had turned up after thirteen years. By the pier. The police had done all the necessaries and they knew it was him. They think he'd fallen and fractured his skull. The tide would have washed him out to sea. She said she was lucky. The tide brought him back.

I still have my secret. She thinks he was playing and he fell. Playing. I don't want to tell her he may have been running. Chased. Running. Scared.

Robin. I miss you. Every day. I know I was afraid because you were so unhappy. I know that made it worse. I haven't always had the best of health – mentally, myself and I couldn't bear to see you depressed and know I couldn't help . . . I don't know why you had to go away. Robin?

Hold on STELLA, *then a pool of light on the bed.*

CHRISTINE *sits down and clutches the newspaper to her chest.*

CHRISTINE. It's ok. He didn't hate me. I have him now, I have him for ever . . .

Music: 'There Is A Light That Never Goes Out' by The Smiths.

The Missing Children images are repeated on the back wall.

CHRISTINE *sings along with the chorus:*

There is a light and it never goes out,
There is a light and it never goes out, *etc.*

Lights down.

The End.

UNSUSPECTING SUSAN

Stewart Permutt

In memory of Dan Crawford

Characters

SUSAN CHESTER
POLICEMAN (*non-speaking*)
POLICEWOMAN (*non-speaking*)

Setting

*The play is set in an English village somewhere in North-East
Hampshire. Certainly under a two-hour drive from London, in
the gin-and-Jaguar belt.*

*Most of the action takes place in Susan's living room. She has
lived in this house all her life. It belonged to her parents before
her. It is a solid Georgian building, with five bedrooms, and a
sizeable garden. She has a fine bone structure and very good
deportment. In her youth, Susan would have been considered a
typical English rose. But she is still an attractive woman who
isn't vain about growing old. She sports quite a number of grey
hairs among her fine head of hair. Susan is always neatly and
sensibly dressed. Blouse and skirt and a good pair of walking
shoes. She is articulate and speaks in those rather nice dulcet
tones that can still be heard along the country lanes in the
Home Counties.*

*The living room is rather cluttered. There are several pieces of
really good antique furniture, with bookcases piled high with
books and piles of books on the floor. Stage left is a church
pew where the only other action in the play takes place.*

Unsuspecting Susan was first presented by Harold Sanditen for Sandpiper Theatre Productions Ltd at the King's Head Theatre, Islington, London, on 6 May 2003, and subsequently as part of the Brits Off Broadway season at 59E59 Theaters, New York, on 14 June 2005, with the following cast:

SUSAN   Celia Imrie

Director   Lisa Forrell
Designer   Nigel Hook
Lighting Designer   Cosmo Lumiere
Lighting Designer (US)   David Kidd
Composer   Edmund Butt
Dramaturg   Phil Setren

Scene One

Early evening on a fine spring day in April 2002. Before the
lights come up we hear a hymn which has particular relevance
to the time of year. This fades as the lights come up on
SUSAN.

SUSAN. It's a wonderful view out of this window, isn't it? You
can see right across the green to the . . . The Crooked Mile.
You can even smell them cooking the Sunday roast from my
kitchen window and they grow their own veg. To be honest
with you, now I'm on my own, I often pop in there after
church for a spot of lunch. I don't care what Delia Smith says,
cooking for one can be bloody miserable . . . This is actually
two houses knocked together. My father bought it in 1948 for
a song, now everybody tells me I'm sitting on a small fortune,
but I've no intention of moving until they cart me off to the
graveyard at the back of the church.

A young couple have bought the place next door. They seem
perfectly all right, she's a social worker of all things. I'd never
have taken her for a social worker in a million years . . . Spiky
hair and patent-leather pixie boots, but she specialises in
children who commit violent crimes. 'You're going to find us
rather dull here, I'm afraid. The most controversial thing that
happens is who's chosen to read the lesson. Are you church-
going people?' I asked. 'No, we're agnostic.' I've always believed
that people have to find their own way. Elaine Sweetham, you
know, Donald Sweetham's wife, has turned to Buddhism since
she's discovered Donald's been unfaithful. I'm afraid it's been
common knowledge in the village for ages but Elaine, bless
her, was the last to know. I thought I'm damned if I tell her and
I'm damned if I don't, so I didn't. 'Elaine, I'm at the other end
of the tunnel once you've come through.' But she said meditation
has changed her life. She met some guru in Farnham and he's
moved in apparently. It's just a phase she's going through. My
son's been through every phase and fad you could possibly
imagine but he's so much better now.

I wasn't terribly happy about him going to live in London. I try
to avoid London as much as possible these days . . . you wouldn't
believe the people I saw in Harrods last time I went . . . as
Mummy would say: 'Strictly N.Q.O.C.D.' . . . Not Quite Our
Class Darling . . . No, I wouldn't say I was a bit of a snob, I'd
say I was a tremendous snob. My mother said it was the thin
end of the wedge when her butcher went to Majorca. But I
must say I've quite taken to that new social worker. She's
promised to give me a whole load of her dirndl skirts for the
church jumble sale. She says she welcomes the tranquillity of
this place after a gruelling day at work. They've still kept up a
little bolt-hole in London . . . in Pimlico. I said my son's living
in Victoria but I doubt whether they would have come across
him. London's such a huge place. It gets more frightening
every time I go there. But Simon seems much more settled.
He's living with a very nice young man. They're just flatmates.
I'm quite pleased because the thing about Simon is he never
made friends very easily. He always wanted to stay at home
with me, rather than be out playing cricket on the green. But
then he's very sensitive. I'd like to say he took after his father.
But Colin never amounted to anything. I can't think why I ever
married him in the first place. He was quite good-looking if
you go for that sort of thing, but an absolute bastard. I'm sorry
but he is. I was at a friend's wedding when suddenly the
heavens opened, he was standing at the other side of the lawn
and he rushed over to shelter me under his umbrella. He was
dark and handsome . . . but only five foot six otherwise he
could have stepped straight out of one of Barbara Cartland's
novels. A real charmer but a compulsive liar, spun me a yarn
about being a property developer. He's never had two pennies
to rub together. But I was a very naive young girl then and
believed everything people told me. Simon's only seen his
father three times since the divorce and two of those occasions
was when Colin wanted to borrow money. He's inherited his
father's looks and I know one day he's going to make some
girl very happy.

I was telling that social worker all about Simon's mood
swings. Funny I've only known her five minutes but once you
get beyond the spiky hair there's a very sympathetic face. He
used to just lock himself in his bedroom and not come out for

days or even weeks. Said he was in this great black hole and there was no way out and that hell was waiting just around the corner. Elaine Sweetham is heading along the same path if she's not careful; believe me, I know the signs. Mummy never believed in depression or nerves or anything like that . . . She was quite a character. Everyone in the village adored her. She had that wonderful knack of treating everyone as though they were equal. She used to send steam puddings and home-made jams to the wives down on the estate, when their husbands were laid off. I've carried on the tradition.

My father was a doctor but he didn't help Simon. He never quite understood him. When he was at his lowest ebb, all Daddy did was prescribe very small dosages of Valium. He was a very conscientious doctor, said the countryside was littered with poor unfortunate housewives addicted to Valium. He'd bury himself in his surgery at the back of the house and we only saw him on Sundays and holy days.

She starts to arrange some framed photos on the sideboard. She picks up one and looks at it.

This was taken of Simon on his twenty-first birthday outside The Crooked Mile with just me and Elaine. She's the only person in the village who accepts Simon for who he is.

She puts the photo back.

Everybody else treats him as some kind of leper, just because he's had difficulties. Mental problems are like everything else, you find out what the matter is and then you find a cure . . . it's as simple as that . . . nothing to be ashamed of but people in villages can be very small-minded when it comes to things like that. Alison McNaughton is the worst offender if you ask me. She's chairwoman or chair-person as she likes to call herself, of the women's sub-committee. She's got an opinion about everything and she knows nothing. Had the cheek once to criticise the way I brought Simon up. 'You're letting him run amok, Susan, he doesn't know right from wrong. A bit of firm discipline is what he needs.' Now in my book, there are two things you never pass judgement on and that's other people's children and other people's driving. Alison's never had any children but she does drive . . .

It was after his second suicide attempt that I dragged him kicking and screaming to a very well-known shrink in Harley Street. 'Now don't beat about the bush,' I said. 'Is Simon a schizophrenic or a manic-depressive?' He looked across at me with his horn-rimmed spectacles and said: . . . 'We treat the individual not the symptoms.' He then wrote out a prescription for a new anti-depressant and assured me that Simon's condition was what they call a chemical imbalance, nothing to do with his childhood. He more or less said Freud was a load of old poppycock and I went back on the train feeling rather relieved, I must say.

I'm afraid those tablets didn't work. After only ten days he'd smashed up the conservatory and broken all the downstairs windows. He had to be admitted to hospital. There was no alternative. Although he never laid a finger on me or the dogs. He adores the dogs. He then went on this course for anger management, he was doing rather well until he hacked my Queen Anne dressing table to pieces with a mallet. I told him these hands were made to create not destroy . . . But he's so much better now he's found his feet in London. He says he hasn't felt suicidal once since he's been there. And he's managed to channel his anger. He's got a real friend in that young man he's sharing with . . . Jamal. Egyptian. Came over here to study engineering. His parents are what you call very liberal. His mother dresses like we do and his father's even been known to have a drink on special occasions, although Jamal's very strict about alcohol. Which I'm rather pleased about because between you and me and the gatepost, Simon's been what they call a substance abuser. I must say they've made that little flat look very cosy. Some rather good Persian rugs and flowers and candles everywhere. Jamal is the perfect host, not that I ever outstayed my welcome, but he just couldn't do enough for me. And for two boys sharing together, it's spotlessly clean. Simon was always a messy pup so I think it must be Jamal's influence.

'You will keep an eye on Simon, won't you?' I said to Jamal, just as I was about to leave. 'Don't worry, Mrs Chester. He's my brother.' Simon's never had a brother . . . They met at a Blur concert. Tickets were like gold dust, Simon queued all night. They happened to be sitting next to each other and just got chatting, the way people do at concerts.

Simon needs to find something he wants to do. Take a leaf out of Jamal's book. Do a degree or one of those business courses. He's almost thirty-three but it's not too late. One day my coffers are going to run dry and he'll have to support himself. I don't want him ending up like his father. Never held down a job, for ever borrowing money. Always involved in some hare-brained scheme or other. He'd really gone to seed last time I saw him. Frayed shirt collar and dirty old corduroys . . . and he was such a dashing young man in his youth.

I've never thought of marrying again. I've been taken off the shelf a few times, dusted down and put back again but nothing very serious. You see, I'm not what you might call a voracious woman. Between you and me, I don't really like it. Load of fuss and nonsense about nothing. I lead rather a busy life, I'm a landscape gardener by profession. Then there are the dogs. Sealyhams. Used to breed them, now I've just got Sally and Eros. They're both quite old now. Marvellous company, dogs are. Mummy was a dog-mater, you know. She was quite well-known for it up and down the county. Used to trundle around in her old Morris Minor Shooting Brake wearing a pair of elbow-length marigolds and arrive on people's doorstep saying: 'My method never fails . . . could you please vacate the room while I'm affecting the union.' I said: 'Mummy, wouldn't it have been killing if you'd have gone on *What's My Line*? . . . Nobody would have guessed.'

We hear a dog barking.

Sally, be quiet! Bless her. She tried to bite the new postman last week. I expect she had her reasons. I don't know where she gets the energy from. Eros is the exact opposite, he likes the quiet life, like me. I expect he's snuggled up somewhere nice and warm. This is an awfully big house, eleven rooms. It just seems so empty now Simon's not here. But he's finding his feet, that's what's important.

I made the mistake of telling that social worker from next door . . . Louise, or Lou as she likes to be called, rather too much over our first cup of tea. Her husband can hardly string a sentence together but he's very practical, offered to mend the lock on the downstairs loo, so I've decided to be pleasant. But I could tell that Lou was starting to put her professional cap on and all I said was that Simon's got one of those helter-skelter personalities. One minute up and the next down . . . Though it did break my heart when he told me he felt that he was a useless individual, and his life wasn't worth living. They don't give you tablets for that and if they do, we haven't found the right one. Mummy would say: 'That's young people for you, it's nothing but self, self, self, and if there's anything left over then it's self again.' That Lou started bombarding me with questions: 'How often does he see his father?' Not that it's got anything to do with her but the last time Colin visited Simon was when he was in hospital. I had to put a stop to it after that. He told Simon to pull himself together before it was too late. The staff said he'd reduced Simon to tears. If Simon could pull himself together he wouldn't have been there in the first place. Then Louise asked me if Simon had experienced any childhood traumas? . . . Of course he didn't experience any childhood traumas, I was always by his side . . . I would have sent her away with a flea in her ear but her husband went on to fix the sash on my kitchen window. Besides, we need all the able-bodied men we can get on our bell-ringing team. You don't even have to go to church. We have our own social life which has got nothing to do with the women's sub-committee. Alison went up into the belfry and made a right pig's ear out of it. John, he's our captain, won't let her up there again. It's a skill that few can master. I'm the only female campanologist this side of Andover . . . but we're always on the lookout for new recruits, even if they are champagne socialists . . . well, they've got it written all over them . . . Buying expensive property bang in the middle of the gin-and-Jag belt and then spouting off about deprived teenagers in South London. We've got another lefty on the other side of the green . . . Always campaigning on behalf of those immigrants, yet he never lets the girls use his path for the horses.

She goes to the bookshelves, picks up a book and then puts it down.

We had a meeting last week of the Operatic and Dramatic

Society and we've plumped for an all-female production this
year as the men would rather be in the pub. We've got a new
producer which is rather exciting . . . Reg Lynas, retired BBC
radio documentary maker. Alison twisted his arm and he said
he'd do it on one condition: that he can drag the society
kicking and screaming into the twenty-first century. Last year
we did *No, No, Nanette* with no chorus. This year it was a toss-
up between *Come Back Little Sheba*, which is an American
play about a housewife who loses her dog or *The Killing of
Sister George* . . . they made a film of it with Beryl Reid.
Alison was worried that it might offend some of the villagers.
But Reg said it was our duty to shock people and make
them think. So *The Killing of Sister George* was voted in by
nine votes against one. Alison's met her match with Reg . . .
I think she rather assumed she'd be playing the lead . . . June
Buckridge . . . 'Sister George' . . . but Reg just looked at me
and said: 'We've got the perfect George right here.' He said
I had the authority coupled with that essential vulnerability.
Elaine, bless her, said: 'We all still remember Susan's Peter
Pan.' Elaine's going to play Childie . . . my 'special friend',
and Alison's agreed to take a supporting role as Mrs Croft, the
lady from the BBC . . . I might rope in that social worker to
help out with the costumes, it'll be a way of introducing her to
everyone in the village, providing she keeps her politics to
herself.

The lights fade.

Scene Two

One month later.

SUSAN. Terry, our local bobby, called in just a minute ago. He
said he didn't want to frighten me but he thinks this house is in
a vulnerable position and there's been one or two robberies
recently. And was I being extra vigilant about locking windows
and doors? I told him not to worry, Sally and Eros would make
a frightful din if anyone as much as came near the place.
Terry's been popping in quite a lot recently, he said would I
give his regards to Simon if I was seeing him and how pleased

he was that he was finally on the straight and narrow as it were. Wanted to know if Simon was living on his own, I mentioned he had a flatmate but I didn't go into details. People can get the wrong end of the stick sometimes . . . Simon never liked Terry but then he had a thing about authority.

Elaine's now officially split up with Donald. He's living with this trollop that works in a betting shop in Basingstoke. Elaine says she's fifty if she's a day. 'I could understand if he'd traded me in for a younger model, but not some old boiler like that. What does he see in her?' 'She's a tart' . . . I said. 'Men go for that sort of thing.'

She said she'd be in the gutter if it wasn't for Buddhism. Every time she feels this uncontrollable hatred towards Donald or the Basingstoke tart, she meditates and becomes calm and full of joy and happiness. But her guru has told her not to become attached to this state because it's not permanent. I wonder if that guru sees himself as permanent . . . I knew there was no going back when she told me that Alison McNaughton's lurcher was her mother in a former life.

Reg is at his wits' end, we open with *Sister George* in three-and-a-half weeks and Elaine doesn't know a word of it. She might just as well not be there. Reg said if she doesn't knuckle under he's going to have to replace her. He's quite a taskmaster but I find it invigorating. He lent me a copy of *An Actor Prepares* . . . 'Let this be your bible, Susan.' He said the secret of good acting is to allow the audience right at the back of the hall to see the interior life of your character. Elaine just whispers it all, it's very irritating. Reg wants us to do some research. You know what the subject matter is . . . he fears we may not have had any first-hand experience, living in a small village like this. That's where I've got a head-start on everyone. Quite a few years ago, before Elaine or Alison were here, there were two spinsters who lived in the little cottage by the stream. Miss Wiggins and Miss Winkler. We used to call them 'The Tiggywinklers'. Miss Wiggins must have stood six foot two in her stocking feet. Her father was the local bobby, I think he used to hit her that's why she ended up hating men. She always carried a bit of a torch for my mother and when Mummy died, poor Miss Wiggins was seen lurking behind a tree, watching the cortège go by, too upset to come to the funeral.

Reg isn't very happy with Alison either, he says she knows her lines and doesn't bump into the furniture, but there's nothing going on underneath.

It's up to me to hold the fort but I've got things on my mind which I try not to bring to rehearsals. Last time I went to see Simon he had that worried look in his eyes, always a sign that he's under the weather. Though I must say he's been on a very even keel. I'm probably worrying unnecessarily. I haven't said a word to Jamal about Simon's mood swings . . . there hasn't been any need . . . after all, he's just someone Simon met at a concert. He reminds me a bit of Colin . . . an absolute charmer . . . until I got to know him.

I don't think Simon's eating properly. I should imagine Jamal goes in for all that spicy food. Simon likes plain cooking. He's used to seeing something on his plate that he can recognise . . . not covered in some disgusting sauce . . . I always come laden with home-made quiches that can just be popped in the oven, but I'm never quite sure they get eaten.

The lease is up and the landlord is putting up their rent. They've been looking around but you've no idea how expensive London is these days. It's not good for Simon to be uprooted. I'm rather worried but I tried not to show it.

I caught them in the middle of packing up the pictures and carpets and all of Jamal's lovely ornaments. He's got these beautiful sets of Egyptian cotton sheets, and a wardrobe full of clothes that I'm sure he's never worn. A friend has offered them storage space, said he could sleep on his floor till they find somewhere. Neither of them could remember this friend's address off-hand but Simon promised he'd ring me with it. Seems criminal when I've got this great big house, they could stay here at least until they find somewhere, but Jamal needs to be near the university. He speaks four languages. And he has to be near a mosque. We've never discussed religion before, although at the end of the day, if we all respected and understood each other a little more, then there wouldn't be all these conflicts . . . I meekly said that there is only one God. And

Jamal smiled gently and said: 'Yes, there is only one God.'
I thought we were sharing something rather deep at that
moment. His father is quite ill and he said when his parents
become too old and frail to look after themselves then it will
be his duty as a Muslim to look after them. Jamal and I may be
of different faiths but I felt we shared the same principles
regarding family ties and morality . . . But the Jesus of the
Koran is described as a prophet of God, he predicts the coming
of Mohammed, but they don't think he is the son of God.

That was two weeks ago and I haven't heard from Simon.
I wish I knew where they were staying. His mobile seems to be
permanently switched off but I'm not unduly worried. He'll
contact me when they've settled in somewhere. I often don't
hear from Simon for weeks on end . . . that's sons for you,
isn't it? I'm not going to do anything drastic this time because
I know he's perfectly all right . . . But one phone call is all I
ask.

She picks up a piece of embroidery.

I promised Ian . . . that's our new vicar . . . that I'd have these
ready for Trinity Sunday. They're a pair of kneelers for the
church pews. They're in memory of my old sheepdog Bessie.
She's buried at the bottom of the garden. Sally and Eros are
getting on a bit and when they go I don't think I'll have any
more animals. I can't bear burying them. After all, I'm entering
the home-run myself.

She goes towards a decanter of whisky on a side table.

I think I might have the smallest drink you could possibly
imagine, I know it's early and normally I wouldn't but I need
a steady hand this afternoon for the bottling.

She pours a large whisky.

I've made some of my famous damson jam for one of Alison's
coffee mornings. It always goes down a treat.

That Jamal's a very sensible young man. It's as if Simon was
one of his own people. That's the thing about Simon, you can't
really help liking him. When old Mrs Dods used to struggle
across the green with her shopping, Simon was always the first
to help her. The shrink in the last place that he went said he

was a paranoid schizophrenic. Well, all I can say is that when he's not being paranoid and not being schizophrenic, he's a jolly nice person.

She pours herself another whisky as the lights fade.

Scene Three

About one week later.

SUSAN. Elaine didn't turn up for rehearsals yesterday. She wasn't answering the phone. We all got very worried. I said to Reg, 'I'm going round.' I must have been banging on that door for the best part of ten minutes, finally her guru, or whatever he calls himself, answered and said unless it was a matter of life or death, Elaine was meditating. I said 'We open in ten days' time.' He said: 'Let go of it.' I just pushed past him and found Elaine in the lotus position, knee-deep in leftovers from the Chinese take-away. Eventually she transcended to my level and muttered something about the play destroying her karma and that she was on a mission to improve her karma and go to Buddha heaven until her karma runs out and that I was more than welcome to join her. 'I'm sorry, Elaine, but we've got a play to get on.'

'I'm going to London tomorrow with Keith, he's got some friends in Bayswater.'

'Bayswater! London! But what about your little problem?'

'What little problem?' chimed in this Keith.

'It's all right, he knows. Don't you, darling?' . . . said Elaine suddenly becoming all girly and coy, nauseating in a woman of fifty-six.

'Susan, Keith knows all about my irritable bowel syndrome.'

'That was due to stress,' said Keith the Guru. 'Meditation has transferred all her negative feelings into positive energy curing all her symptoms.'

All the same, I hope she remembers to take her 'I.B.S. Can't Wait' card with her . . . It simply states that you're not contagious and gives you carte blanche to knock on people's doors and use their facilties. But will people in Bayswater be as understanding as they are in Hampshire?

As you can imagine, Reg was tearing his hair out in rehearsals. He suggested recruiting somebody from Hook. But for once, Alison and I were in agreement, we very much want to keep this play a parish effort. Then Reg threatened to call the whole thing off. But we've sold all the tickets . . . they've even done an interview with Reg in the *Hampshire News* . . . The reporter said it wasn't his favourite subject matter. Reg accused him of being homophobic and he said some of his best friends were homosexuals but women should know better. Mind you, if I had a daughter I'd feel awfully let down if she was that way inclined. Then I came up with a brilliant idea . . . What about Louise, the social worker? . . . She's the right age for starters. It took some persuading. Although she has done quite a bit of acting when she was at college . . . I guessed as much. Reg said not to worry about the lines, she can go on with the book and she said she'd only do it if she could play Childie as a lipstick lesbian . . . Reg said she could play it as a Red Indian providing she turns up on the night.

The lights fade.

Scene Four

Ten days later.

We hear some music, possibly a light-hearted music-hall song. Lights come up as SUSAN *enters, carrying a bottle of champagne and a large bouquet of flowers. She is flushed after her success in* The Killing of Sister George.

SUSAN. These are from Simon, he didn't forget. Aren't they lovely . . . I'm just going to put them in water.

She disappears for a moment. We hear a tap running, then she returns, holding a card which she reads.

'Sorry I can't be there tonight. Break a leg, Mum, as the saying goes . . . love Simon.' . . . Silly boy, those flowers must have cost him a fortune. That florist in Eelbrook seems to make up her own prices. I can't wait to see them in their new flat. He left a message on my machine . . . the line was a bit crackly . . . didn't leave a number . . . but they've found a place in Willesden . . . Can't tell you what a weight off my mind it is just to hear from him.

She pours herself a whisky.

I think I deserved that. All things being equal, I think we did rather well tonight. Louise, you know, the social worker, threw caution to the wind and did the whole thing without the play in her hand. Which made me look a bit of a charlie, I'm afraid, as most of the time she was making her lines up and I didn't know when to come in with mine. We got ourselves into a right pickle in the second act when we were doing our Laurel and Hardy routine. Jill Greenhalgh was supposed to be prompting but at half-time they found her in the pub on her fourth gin and tonic. But that's Jill all over. First sign of trouble and she's out the door. She won't be getting my vote this year when she stands for Electoral Roll Officer . . . Reg said that despite everything Louise and I had a real feeling between us and that was more important than anything. He reckons she saved the show, which is a bit unfair. But in the pub afterwards, lots of people came up to me and told me I was as solid as a rock.

Jill Greenhalgh was practically on the floor. I'm surprised her husband never says anything . . . I mean, it's not as if it's the first time. As far as I'm concerned she'd let the side down rather badly. Reg said with all this talent floating about on the distaff side he might do *The House of Bernarda Alba* next. Although I know the general consensus is to do another pantomime. We'll never be able to rival our *Jack and the Beanstalk*. I was the Fairy Courgette. I had a little song towards the end.

She launches into her little ditty.

How does the brown cow make white milk
When it only eats green grass?
That's the burning question,
Burns like indigestion . . .

I don't know,
You don't know
Isn't it a crime
Oh . . . how does the brown cow make white milk
When it only eats green grass.

That was such fun . . . Alison played The Spirit Of Evil and
Elaine put on her fishnets and high heels and had a jolly good
stab at Jack. I haven't heard from her since she's gone to
Bayswater. That Zen Buddhism or whatever she calls it has
taken over her life. But when it all goes pear-shaped and she
comes running back, I'll be expected to pick up the pieces as
usual.

The lights fade as SUSAN *pours herself another glass of*
whisky before going to bed. The lights go to black, then
come up again. It is early morning, her house is surrounded
by police cars with lights flashing, but quiet. There is a
knock at the door, we are aware of policemen outside
surveying the garden, etc. There is another loud knock at
the door. Two POLICEMEN *are outside, a man and a*
woman. The lights go from semi-darkness to full up. The
POLICE *enter. Now there are loud police sirens. Then as*
they go down again we hear the shock reverberating in
SUSAN*'s head as we go to complete darkness and stillness.*

Scene Five

One month later.

The lights come up very slowly. SUSAN *is sitting on a church*
pew. She is very subdued. She is rather carelessly dressed, not
her normal neat self from previous scenes. There is a moment
of silence before she speaks.

SUSAN. This is a remarkably beautiful church. That stained-
glass window to the east of blue and white roses was put up to
mark the marriage of King Henry VII to Elizabeth of York in
1486. By the pulpit is a stained-glass window painted by the
Pre-Raphaelite artist Burne-Jones. It's really quite
breathtaking.

She breaks off suddenly.

Ian, our new vicar, is quite a remarkable man. He made me come to church last Sunday, they sang Simon's favourite hymn.

She begins to sing.

'He who would valiant be
'Gainst all disaster
Let him in constancy
Follow the Master . . . '

She breaks off.

Because he was a Christian, you know, despite everything, he was always a Christian. Jesus was important to him.
He believed in taking from the rich to give to the poor and being kind to your neighbour. Ian said that Simon was a poor creature who had lost his way and that Christ was ready to receive him and forgive his sins. John, the bell captain, insisted on using dusters to muffle the bells as a mark of respect. There was quite an outcry from everybody except Jill Greenhalgh of all people, she's been an absolute brick. Poor gin-ridden old Jill is the only person keeping me sane. 'Case of the blind leading the blind, Susan,' she said last night in her cups.

Ian used as his text Matthew 7:

'Judge not that ye be not judged. For with what judgement ye judge, ye shall be judged, and with what measure ye mete, it shall be measured to ye again.'

I just crept in late at the back and then crept out early before anyone could see me. Ian said, 'This is your church and you are a very valued member of the community.' I had to resign as treasurer of the parish council although Ian made it quite clear to all and sundry that it was my decision. Alison McNaughton can't look me in the face. Although she had plenty to say to those reporters who've descended on the village like a plague of locusts. Most days I can't go out the door, they're hiding in the bushes or behind the old oak tree. Devious creatures . . . the women are the worst . . . they pretend to be sympathetic. Jill's taught me to say: 'No comment,' then they can't misquote you. Alison's had a field day. She's been inviting them in for coffee and home-made cakes . . . I know she never liked me but the picture she's painted to the tabloids about me and Simon is quite false. According to her I was this terribly possessive mother who would let him vandalise property without punishing him and the whole sorry state of events could have been prevented by a firm hand in early childhood. Jill told the press it was just damn bad luck and you can't control your children. One of the papers said that Simon came from a dysfunctional family . . . I've a good mind to sue. The word dysfunctional's banded about a lot these days. Look at Jill's two boys. She's hardly what you would call a perfect mother, and one's a financial consultant and the other's a big noise in the dot-com world. So don't talk to me about dysfunctional families.

She is almost about to cry, then checks herself, kneels down beside the pew for a few seconds of silent prayer. She gets up and moves out of the church and we hear her open her front door with a key, enter through her hallway into her living room as the lights come up. The curtains are drawn. There is the feeling that the place hasn't been dusted for some time. There are several boxes on the floor piled high with toys, etc. SUSAN immediately goes and pours herself a large drink from the decanter.

Jill's started going to the happy-clappy church in Eelbrook: 'I've never been hugged and kissed so much in my life,' she said. 'I wonder what they do to people they really like . . . '

Now Elaine's been banished to Bayswater, I don't know what I'd do without Jill. She's in the middle of writing the definitive book on divorce, called *Turn off the Sprouts, I'm Leaving*. I'm afraid I put the phone down on Elaine last night, I know she was trying to be helpful but all this bloody claptrap she was coming out with about Simon being punished for something he did in a former life and then him being reborn as some beautiful free spirit . . . I don't want him reborn, I want him with me now.

She takes a large sip of whisky.

Jill Greenhalgh uttered the one bit of common sense when she said that this was our only true friend.

She goes over to the boxes and takes out a teddy bear.

They took this away for forensics, then they gave it back to me. There's a big hole at the back which they stitched back again, and all the stuffing's been taken out . . . What were they hoping to find?

She hugs the bear.

He's had it since he was a baby. He wanted to take him with him when he went to London, but I said we'll keep Mister Scruffy in your bedroom for when you come home. I'm going to put it in the coffin with Simon when they let me have him back.

She puts the bear back again.

I was about to go to bed when the police came, they surrounded the place. The garden, the shed, everywhere. They'd been there all night but I didn't know. It was about four o'clock in the morning when they knocked on the door. They showed me their IDs. Anti-terrorist branch. A young woman, pretty, blonde, could have been my daughter and two others, can't remember much about them other than they completely ransacked the place . . . first Simon's room, they just took everything away in huge sacks . . . then they went through my entire house . . . you know how it feels when you've been burgled . . . they went through all the papers in my study and my china and dismantled that lovely silver service that was a wedding present from Mummy and Daddy . . . I can't bear to touch it now . . . they sifted through my laundry and took down all the books from the shelf . . . I feel as if everything has been contaminated. First I thought it was some kind of practical joke, and in pretty poor taste, but we were all a bit high after the play and some people round here have got a very quaint sense of humour.

The pretty, blonde policewoman . . . Karen is her name . . . too young and pretty for this sort of work, I thought, sat me down. 'Mrs Chester, I wish to speak to you regarding a matter involving your son,' she said in a nice clear voice. They have special training for this sort of work. 'Has he been involved in some sort of accident?' . . . 'We are investigating a terrorist incident which took place last night at a restaurant in the West

End of London at 9.35 pm. You may have heard about it on the news?' . . . News, I haven't listened to the news, I was doing *The Killing of Sister George* . . . 'I'm afraid I have some bad news,' said the poor girl who could have been my daughter. 'Your son has been killed and we have reason to believe he is the person who perpetrated the crime . . . ' 'This is some terrible mistake, it can't be my son, he sent me a beautiful bouquet of flowers, they're over there.' The nice young policewoman looked at them admiringly, took my hand and said, 'His body is at the police mortuary in London, we'd like it if you'd come with me to identify him.' 'Let's not waste any more time, it's all some dreadful mistake.' I kept on repeating, hoping they'd go away. Then the place seemed to be swarming with police, I don't know where they came from. I felt sick and D.C. Karen took me into the kitchen and made me a cup of tea. It was sort of comforting but my mouth felt numb. She didn't say anything for a long time. It's part of their training. Then she told me that Simon and that friend of his had been under surveillance for some time. The police had taken some things from their flat in Victoria . . . 'Taken!' I said . . . 'You can't go breaking into people's flats without a warrant.' . . . 'It's something we do all the time, I'm afraid, Mrs Chester.' We took a sample from your son's hairbrush, then it was sent away for analysis, so we had it on file. Then last night we took a sample away with us from the body of the bomber and it matched up with your son's.'

It was a suicide bombing in a Jewish restaurant in London. Five people were killed, including a woman who was six months pregnant and an elderly couple celebrating their diamond wedding. The old woman died in the ambulance and he died just as they got to hospital. One little girl is so badly burnt that she's already had to have two skin transplants . . . there's been pictures of her in the papers, I can't look . . . I see her in my dreams, when I lie awake at night . . . and . . .

She stops before she can utter the names of the others.

I had to identify Simon's body. They said it was better to get it over with. D.C. Karen said she'd go with me and all the time I convinced myself that it wouldn't be Simon lying there, you know how you do, that it was all a mistake and I'd go home and

that would be that . . . That car journey seemed to take for ever.
I was hoping we'd never arrive . . . But it wasn't a mistake . . .
no . . . it wasn't a mistake . . . they took the sheet off and it
was him! Oh God help me it was him! My baby . . . it was him!
Yes . . . Bits of chandelier were burnt right into his skin . . .
They'd stitched his head together at the back so I could
identify him . . . my little boy lying there, stitched together with
great lumps of glass burnt to his flesh . . . but it was him . . .
Oh God . . . I went into a little room and was sick and I tried to
scream but nothing happened no matter how I tried, and Karen
held my hand and didn't say anything and I wanted to hug him
and say everything's all right like I used to. But they wouldn't
let me take him home with me, so I can't even bury him,
though John muffled the bells last Sunday as a sign of respect.

It wasn't Simon who did that . . . I know it was him but it
wasn't him, he was possessed by those evil people. The police
said it was an exact replica of the suicide bombings in the
Middle East and they believe that Simon was working for
some organisation. Jamal was part of it . . . That charming
young man who served me tea out of a beautiful copper pot.

They talked of a military academy in Afghanistan where they
trained terrorists. They said it bore all the hallmarks of a
known organisation. It was a very professional job, Simon
knew exactly what he was doing . . . but he didn't, that's what I
tried to tell them.

When we got back, D.C. Karen asked me if I was up to
answering a few questions. 'How close was Jamal to your son?'
she asked . . . 'Close,' I said. 'They were just flat-mates.' . . .
'Do you think there may have been something deeper?' . . .
'Simon and Jamal got on very well if that's what you mean.' . . .
'No,' said Karen . . . 'We mustn't rule out the possibility that
they were more than just good friends.' . . . More than just
good friends . . . How ridiculous . . . Simon wasn't that way
inclined . . . I wouldn't have minded if he was, one must be
true to oneself . . . besides, that kind of thing carries a death
penalty where Jamal comes from. Though I told them I'd do
anything to help them find the man who had brainwashed
my baby. People like that are the scum of the earth . . . D.C.
Karen said that if everyone was as sensible as me, their jobs

would be so much easier. All this time, Simon and that terrible
boy had been under surveillance. My phone's been tapped,
and my neighbours and the local police were in on it . . . that's
why Terry was always popping round. If Jamal had been
under surveillance why hadn't anybody bloody well done
something! . . . But Karen said he hadn't committed any crime.
All they knew was that Jamal was part of some extremist
organisation that preyed on vulnerable young men like Simon.
There are cells operating all over London . . . even in Bayswater.
People like Jamal trap innocent boys like Simon to do their
dirty work. They're very clever, they don't use phones or
computers, it's impossible to trace anything. She reckons they
must have met at the mosque. And Simon told me they'd sat
next to each other at a Blur concert.

She picks up an article in the box belonging to Simon.

One Guy Fawkes night . . . Simon was only eight, we'd invited
everyone over for a big bonfire party, and Simon just went over
and set fire to this huge pile of fireworks just where one of
Jill's boys was standing. I saw it in the nick of time, pulled the
child out of the way, stamped on the fireworks . . . but it could
have been very nasty . . . Everyone thought it was an accident.
But I knew it wasn't an accident. I saw Simon deliberately go
over to that pile of fireworks and set them alight. I never said
a word to him, you know what boys are like. He needed help
even then and I did nothing. D.C. Karen said the bomb was
stuffed down one of Simon's boots when he went into that
restaurant. A professional job, she said.

That social worker Louise has been dishing out her
professional advice left, right and centre. I don't answer the
door to her now, I think she's got the message . . . Colin's
going to appear in a documentary on Channel Four, he'll do
anything for money but I won't have anything to do with it.
Has he thought for one moment how it's going to make him
look? No doubt Alison's self-righteous, pinched little face will
be popping up to tell the nation what can go wrong when a
child isn't disciplined.

I've only just found out that Simon was in contact with Colin
all the time he was in London. If I'd known, I'd have made

him come home with me . . . If only I had . . . Louise was
telling me about this self-help group for families of people
who've committed horrific crimes. But the last thing I want to
do is listen to a room full of miseryguts whinging away . . .
Simon did not commit a crime. He was brainwashed. You must
remember the Stockholm Syndrome. A group of ordinary
decent people got on a train one day with a bunch from some
crackpot political group and by the end of that journey those
ordinary decent people had joined up with those hot-headed
crackpots.

She takes another sip of whisky.

Anyone can be influenced by anybody. I was completely taken
in by that Jamal. Anyone would be. He was so charming.
There's a massive search going on for him at the moment. He
could be anywhere in the world and he's very dangerous. He
certainly got my baby to do his dirty work . . . Didn't he? . . .
Simon wrote me a letter, it arrived that day. They took it away
for forensics.

'When you get this letter, you'll know what has happened. It's
the most beautiful thing I've ever done and as you're reading
this, I'll be in heaven. Remember this world is but a passing
shadow, the next life is the one.' It was quite a long letter over
two pages but he ended it with just . . . 'See you there . . . Your
darling Simon.'

They won't even let me have that . . . Elaine said she's waiting
to enter nirvana . . . or Buddhist heaven or whatever she likes
to call it. She said I could join her and the Guru if I just let go.
'No war has ever been fought in the name of Buddhism,' she
said as I slammed the phone down on her.

. . . I wanted to write to the families of those poor Jewish
people that were killed, but I just don't know what to say . . .
Sorry isn't enough, is it? . . . I never brought Simon up to hate
the Jews, or anybody for that matter. I've always had a quiet
admiration for Israel. To begin with, that is. It was such a
pioneering young country, one had to hand it to them after all
they'd been through. Daddy never quite understood how they
all just meekly marched to their deaths without kicking up
some sort of fuss or other. I said, Daddy, it's all very well to

say that but we weren't there at the time. Louise sides with what she sees as the victims or the underdogs . . . the Palestinians . . . She said that the state of Israel was formed by a terrorist act and the rest of the world stood by because they felt guilty about what had happened. She isn't anti-semitic but Israel has got a lot to answer for . . . She understood exactly where Simon's anger was coming from . . . Simon always stood up for the underdog . . . And one way or another the Palestinians have had a pretty rotten deal . . . And the thing about the Jews, however much one may respect them . . . well . . . They've always managed to get exactly what they want . . . haven't they . . . I know I shouldn't say this but you'd be hard put to find a poor Jew these days. They always seem to climb right to the top of the tree. It's the same in the Middle East. They think they can just trample all over the Palestinians and nobody dare say anything . . . Well, it isn't right, is it? . . . I mean, of course nobody should have died or been hurt but sometimes you're forced to do something drastic to prove a point . . . aren't you . . .

I got a very nice letter from the chairman of the mosque Simon had attended. The chairman . . . Abdul . . . Muquaddim . . . something or other . . . said how fond he was of Simon and what a caring member of the community he was . . . Simon had converted, apparently. Abdul said that his mosque is a place of worship and he had always discouraged any extremist views . . . He's asked me to come and visit him. But I can't go to London.

If he was unhappy he could have come home at any time. He didn't have to join some mosque. I loved him. He knew that. I still love him . . . No, he's not a monster . . . And yes, I am going to write to the families of the victims, Louise is right, it will make me feel better. I'm going to sit down now and compose a letter to each and every one of them.

Simon had everything a boy could possibly want. I scrimped and saved to send him to the best school in the area . . . Yes, he did play truant for nearly a year but those sort of places put an awful lot of pressure on you to succeed. He had very unusual taste in music for a boy his age . . . Used to play Billie Holiday in his room all night, I'm afraid I found it rather depressing.

I like music to be uplifting, even at times like this. If it wasn't for the dogs and Jill, I think I might have put my head in the oven. Last time I went down the high street, people ducked into doorways as soon as they saw me, so I've been going into the supermarket in Hook for my bit of shopping. Ian's begged me to come to the 'Après Evensong' at The Crooked Mile, but people won't know what to say, least of all Alison McNaughton despite her crash-course in bereavement counselling.

It's windows Simon would destroy and conservatories and furniture, but not pretty little girls and elderly couples celebrating their diamond wedding . . . he wouldn't hurt them . . .

The lights fade. We hear a sequence of sounds as if they are going on inside SUSAN'*s head. First we hear church bells ringing very loudly followed by the dogs barking. Then we hear the screech of a car, police sirens. Finally we hear knocking at the door which builds to a crescendo.*

Scene Six

Night. About a fortnight later. A single spot comes up on SUSAN. *She is sitting in her pyjamas and dressing gown, rocking gently backwards and forwards.*

SUSAN. I had to answer the door to Terry, just to let him know I hadn't done something silly. But that's not like me. I've got Sally and Eros to think about. I'm fine, I just want to be left alone. I've been in my jim-jams and my dressing gown for four days. I've just been picking away with what's left in the freezer but I've no appetite . . . Elaine Sweetham's all for me going to live with her and the Guru in Bayswater in their cool cave of bliss. But this is my home, I was born in this village and I'm not going to leave. I've had to put bars on all the downstairs windows but some thug managed to climb up my drainpipe and hurl a brick through my bedroom window . . . They've offered me police protection . . . Someone's crouching in my back garden as we speak. It's Simon's birthday tomorrow . . . he would be thirty-three . . . And his body's lying there in two pieces and they won't let me have him back.

I haven't been able to cry since it all happened, not properly.
Jill said she's never met someone with so much self-control
considering what I've been through. I've never approved of
people wearing their hearts on their sleeves.

I wrote to the mother of the little girl. She wrote back, it was
a horrible letter . . . I should never have written in the first
place . . . She said her little girl is just eight years old and was
the prettiest girl in her class with golden blonde ringlets . . .
but not any more . . . Sometimes even she can't bear to look
at her own child . . . They're suggesting she wears a plastic
mask . . . Her husband has had a nervous breakdown, he hasn't
been back to work. It's their son's Bar Mitzvah in a few
months, they don't think they can face it. She doesn't know
how I could have given birth to such an abominable creature . . .
I tore the letter up. 'I hope he rots in hell' was scrawled across
the bottom. She sent me a picture of her daughter, you know,
before . . . I tore that up . . . 'All the King's horses and all the
King's men couldn't put Humpty together again.'

The lights fade.

Scene Seven

*Three months later. We hear a peal of church bells. The lights
come up on* SUSAN. *The box full of Simon's things has been
cleared away.*

SUSAN. John, the bell captain, popped in today: 'We've got a
wedding in Mattingley next Saturday and we won't be able to
have a full ring without you . . . Can I twist your arm, Susan?'
I didn't like to say no . . . I could just go up the bell tower
without being seen and then disappear again. There are still
reporters snooping about . . . it's yesterday's news but it's so
damned controversial. I still daren't venture into the high
street. I went into Hook yesterday but people still stare. A
young woman pushing a baby buggy screamed: 'Murdering
bitch' and then spat in my face.

It's our church fête next Saturday. My cut-and-come-again
cake won first prize last year . . . Ian wants me to have my own

stall as usual but I've handed the honours to Jill Greenhalgh,
who was under the table last time I spoke to her and I doubt
whether she's crawled up yet. There's a self-help group in
Farnham but it's like red rag to a bull if I as much as mention it.

In six months' time the police say it will be all right for me
to bury my darling in the churchyard next to Mummy and
Daddy . . . Thank God they've been spared all this. They
wouldn't have been able to cope. I'm coping remarkably well
apparently . . . They've offered me counselling and what have
you, but I'm afraid I've told them all to go and take a running
jump. It's not going to bring him back and no, I don't want to
speak to other mothers in similar circumstances, thank you
very much.

I've planned Simon's funeral. His favourite hymns of course.
I shall give a tribute and then readings from Revelations
verses 1-7.

She goes to a bookcase and picks up a Bible from the shelf.

Things are just beginning to get back to normal after all that
disruption from the police.

She opens the passage and reads.

'And God shall wipe away all tears from their eyes
And there shall be no more death
Neither sorrow, nor crying,
Neither shall there be any more pain.'

She replaces the Bible.

Just a quiet funeral for those that knew and loved him. Elaine
will come up from London no doubt. But I'd rather most
people stayed away. Except John and Jill, of course, and I shall
ask that nice policewoman, D.C. Karen . . . He deserves a
proper Christian burial.

Who would have thought that Jill Greenhalgh of all people
would end up being my life-line. Louise, the social worker,
keeps saying that if I need any support I only have to ask.
'I know what you're going through,' she said. 'No, you don't.'
And I just walked away.

Jill and I muddle along quite nicely, thank you. I take the dogs for a walk, then we do our errands and then batten down the hatches and have a cosy little drink and a chat . . . Scrambled eggs on toast at about six . . . *The Archers* at seven . . . You'd be surprised how the day just flies by. Jill hasn't spoken to her two boys for nearly a year, she doesn't even know if one of them's still in the country . . . but at least they're alive . . . I keep on thinking I must pop down to London to see if Simon's all right, then I remember . . . They say it'll get easier but it won't . . . How can it? I hear him playing in his room, sometimes I see him at the foot of the stairs. I know I'm not mad, it's just grief but it won't go away. Maybe I don't want it to.

She is about to cry but stops herself.

That's enough of that.

They still haven't caught that terrible boy . . . The one that made Simon do that dreadful thing. It says in the Koran that to kill one innocent human being is like killing all Humanity . . . It doesn't make sense.

She picks up a letter.

Ian thinks I should contact the chairman of the mosque . . . Abdul . . . the one who wrote me that nice letter . . . Says it will help me, someone who knew Simon during the last few months. Someone who appreciated him. I'd like to ask Abdul down here for tea but the trouble is, I just suspect everybody . . . I know it's ridiculous. The other day in Hook two women were walking down the high street wearing those scarves, perfectly ordinary decent Muslim women, I'm sure, but I crossed to the other side . . .

This morning I woke up and couldn't move my legs . . . they'd become paralysed . . . but then I heard the dogs barking and I managed to crawl out of bed.

D.C. Karen said was there anything that could give them a clue when they were piecing together what they call a 'profile' on Jamal. She said if anything came to mind, no matter how trivial, don't hesitate to call. And, you know, I couldn't think of anything at all, no telltale clues. He was always so bloody charming. And Karen said: 'That's part of their armour these days . . . ' Very intelligent girl for a policewoman.

She said she's no psychologist but Simon had just got into the wrong company . . .

She picks up a quilt she has being working on.

I've started a new quilt. One can't control one's life but one can control a quilt.

The dogs haven't been the same . . . They sensed something was wrong straightway . . . Sally's lost her spirit, it's downhill all the way for a Sealyham after that . . . I'll take them out in a minute. I always encouraged Simon's love of animals. What with one thing or another, I had a pretty appalling childhood, but I never so much as harmed a fly. After all, I'm not to blame . . . am I?

The lights fade very slowly with SUSAN *in a single spot as the lights fade to a blackout.*

The End.